THE NEW CLAY

TECHNIQUES AND APPROACHES TO JEWELRY MAKING

by
Nan Roche

with Photography by Chris Roche
and Illustrations by Sue Roche

Flower Valley Press
Rockville, Maryland

Printed and Bound in Hong Kong

ISBN 0-9620543-2-1

10 9 8 7 6 5 4 3 2 1

DEDICATION

To Kathleen Dustin

who introduced me to this wonderful material,

to my husband John,

my friend, partner and supporter of all my myriad pursuits,

and to the memory of our friend Deno Kontos.

END PAPERS: The end papers are a collection of sample pieces made by Kathleen Amt using polymer clay. They were designed to illustrate a knitting book by Lee Anderson.

CONTENTS

Acknowledgements IX

Foreword XIII

Chapter I   INTRODUCTION 1
  The Aim of This Book
  Background
  What is it?

Chapter II   THE BASICS 7
  The Different Brands
  Safety Notes
  Storage
  Baking

Chapter III   TOOLS 15
  Hands
  Surfaces
  Cutting Tools
  Piercing Tools
  Texturing Tools
  Rolling Tools
  The Food Processor

Chapter IV   COLOR 21
  The Color Wheel
  The Primary and Secondary Colors
  Hue, Value and Intensity
  Complementary Colors and Color
  Harmony
  Contrast
  Strategies for Color Mixing

Chapter V   DESIGN 27
  Proportion
  Shape
  Value

Depth
Color
Texture/Pattern

Chapter VI   GETTING STARTED **33**
Clay Preparation
Marble and Imitation of Natural Materials

Chapter VII   BASIC SHAPES **37**

The Ball: Formation & Techniques **38**
The Log or Snake
How to Roll an Even Snake
Cutting the Log
Piercing Beads
Different Piercings
Techniques
Freeform Design
Surface Decoration
Wrap Beads
Your First Cane
Filler Beads
Folded Beads
Checkerboard
Candy Canes: Techniques
Surface Decorations
Disk Beads
Shells

The Sheet: Use and Formation **53**
Sheet Formation
Freeform Folding
Flatwork
Marquetry
Jellyrolls
Stripes and Plaids
Simple Stripes
Pinwheel
Plaid
Splicing
Chevrons
Color Shading
Feathering
Checkerboards
Seminole Patchwork
Mokume Gane
Techniques with Logs and Sheets
Wrapping
Cut and Insert Technique

Chapter VIII   THE CANE AND LOAF **75**
    Simple Canes
    Composite Canes
    Reduction
    A Pattern Cane
    Figure and Face Canes
    Techniques
    The Star
    Fish Scales
    The Flower
    The Face
    Signature Cane

Chapter IX   SURFACE TREATMENTS **89**
    Texture
    Chasing
    Stamping
    Surface Materials
    Paints
    Glitters and Powders
    Metal Foils
    Transfers
    Molding

Chapter X   COLLAGE **97**

Chapter XI   SCULPTURE **103**
    The Human Form
    Caneworking and Building Figures
    Bas-Relief
    3-Dimensional Dolls
    Armatures
    Peoplemaking
    Stuffed Dolls
    Vessels
    Slabworking
    Sheets
    Coiling and Pinching

Chapter XII   FINDINGS and ADDITIONAL APPLICATIONS **117**
    Books
    Bracelets
    Buttons
    Wall Pieces
    Findings
    Necklaces
    Pins and Earrings
    Other Applications

AFTERWORD **125**

APPENDIX **127**

    About Plastics & Hazards

    Selected Bibliography

    Glossary

    Artists Listing

    Suppliers

FOOTNOTES **142**

INDEX **143**

1. A collection of Venetian glass lampworked beads ranging in size from 1/2 to 3".

Acknowledgements

Although polymer clay has been around for a least 40 years, and has been known to dollmakers and miniaturists for many of those years, it is a relatively new material to artists in other media. In the last five to seven years, in conjunction with a resurgence of interest in jewelry and wearable art, the material has "taken off." For this we have to thank a small group of artists on the East and West coasts who have done wonderful work and shared their enthusiasm and ideas.

I was introduced to polymer clay by Kathleen Dustin in her first workshop at the Torpedo Factory Art Center in Alexandria, VA. I will never forget her enthusiasm and wonderful generosity as a teacher. That night I went home so excited I stayed up all night working with the clay. Since then she has continued to teach and inspire artists not only in the Washington area but all across the country through her articles in Ornament Magazine and Craft.

There are two other people who deserve special mention in this regard.

Pier Voulkos, whose necklace was brought to Washington, D.C. from New York by Helen Banes, was seminal in Kathleen's return to working in the media and hence to my introduction to it. At the time, Helen was the president of The Bead Society of Greater Washington and also a member of the Torpedo Factory Art Center along with Kathleen. The two got together to discuss the mysterious makeup of the beads in Pier's necklace. Thus began a landslide of interest and excitement in our area and nationwide. At this writing, plans are in progress for the formation of a Polymer Clay Guild to promote the use of the polymer clays as a serious art media.

Above all, I would like to thank Helene and Seymour Bress for formulating the idea for this book and for having the faith and confidence in me to write it. There certainly would be no book without their support, patience and gentle tutelage. I would never have considered the proposition on my own and it has been a rewarding and exciting adventure.

In the process of writing this book, I have discovered what a highly collaborative effort writing a book really is. I have been only a conductor of many people's efforts on behalf of this project. My family members and friends have spent untold creative, and sometimes frustrating hours working on the book. Without their creativity and energy, there would not have been this book.

The beautiful photography was done by Chris Roche, my brother. Half of it was done in one whirlwind week in San Francisco at his studio. It was an enormous task that many would have said was impossible, involving the works of over 20 artists which had been shipped to his studio and which remained there, sight unseen, until we were ready to photograph it. While I, John Bender (my husband), Sara Richter and Anne Meissner unpacked, grouped and arranged all the items, Chris manned the camera almost non-stop for four days. It was almost the hardest I have ever worked in my life, and my dear brother hung in there with me throughout, matching me two for one. Sara was wonderful, as the creative energy behind the arrangements of the artwork for photography. That is a very time consuming and exacting art that requires great patience and stamina. Sara emerged with idea after wonderful idea for the photos with her fresh approach to each collection of pieces. Many times, when I was utterly exhausted, she still found the energy to keep at it. Anne Meissner was frequently on the scene and spent many hours brainstorming and arranging objects along side Sara. The task would have been insurmountable without them. The other half of the photos were done by Chris and Sara alone, keeping in touch with me by phone and UPS. The process absorbed many of their precious weekends.

A book of this kind would be impoverished and, in some cases unintelligible, without illustrations. Sue Roche, my mother, did all of those required for this book. With nearly 70 illustrations, each requiring many hours to complete, it was an immense task. With a background as a painter and a fine artist, the illustrations required working out a whole new set of techniques and problems. In addition to the hours at the drawing board, many hours were spent on the phone, editing and clarifying the drawings for content and readability. At times it seemed that the job would never end, with new illustrations arriving in the mail regularly. In addition to the enormous effort spent on the illustrations, mother also found the time to organize and draft the chapter on design and edit the color section. The design section would not exist without her persistent encouragement, as the task seemed overwhelming to me. Her knowledge of both color and design were invaluable and form a very significant contribution to the book.

The process of editing and criticizing a book is an unsung and difficult task that adds the polish to it. I was honored to have seven wonderful editors helping me throughout. Four of my editors, Gail Gorlitz, Pamela Dillard, Marty Amt and my husband, John, who had no prior working experience with the clay, proved tremendously helpful in picking up inconsistencies. Three others, Kathleen Dustin, Jamey Allen and Kathleen Amt were the experts I called upon and each had much to add to the information provided and its presentation. Each had a particular emphasis in editing and all spent many, many hours pouring through the manuscript. The book would be significantly diminished without their input.

A special thanks goes to my dear friend Gail. From the very inception of the project, Gail recognized the need to do a hands-on edit of the techniques I described. She kept her involvement with the clay to a minimum until it was time to follow the instructions I had written. It was an enormous task which took several months of her time. Without her enthusiasm and encouragement, I would never have had a hands-on edit done, believing it to be too much to ask of anyone. Well, I was wrong and the book would have suffered without it. She also edited the text for readability and was the first person to read through the manuscript, a scary time for me, through which she was wonderfully supportive and encouraging.

Pamela, who is a wonderful writer, brought a level of language precision to the text that had eluded me. Jamey's editing focused on the discrepancies in the text between the use of Fimo, his medium, and Sculpey, mine. Kathleen Dustin's comments concerned style and were tremendously valuable. Somehow, she found the time to edit the manuscript in the midst of moving her household to Turkey. Kathy and Marty Amt have been wonderful friends and stalwart supporters from the start. In addition to the hours spent editing the manuscript, Marty spent days photographing mosaics in the Freer Gallery for the book. These rare pieces are seldom seen on display and represent a unique opportunity to expose people to them. Without Marty's persistence and effort, they would be absent from the book. Kathy spent many hours with me discussing ideas and content. Her many suggestions have significantly enriched the book.

Of course, without the artists themselves, there would be no book. It was a delight and a privilege to get to know them all. They spent many hours on the phone with me and freely shared their artistic visions, techniques, and information with me. They entrusted their work to me on blind faith and, to a person, were generous and supportive of this project. Howard and Marie Segal of The Clay Factory, Steven Ford and David Forland of City Zen Cane, Maureen Carlson of Wee Folk Creations and Tony Kohn of the Handcraft Designs were especially helpful with technical tips. Everyone was a delight to talk to, and everyone had something to add to the book. I hope the book will reflect some consensus of their ideas about how to work with polymer clay.

It was particularly fun to be able to see many of the artists' studios and observe them at work. I would like to especially thank Michael Grove, Martha Breen, Jamey Allen, Kathy Amt and Kathleen Dustin for the time spent showing me their studios, and sharing their ideas.

I know there are many wonderful artists in this media whom I have omitted. I would have loved to include everyone. Unfortunately I did not always become aware of many people until it was too late for inclusion. My apologies to all and I hope to see your work in the future. One artist in particular I searched for without success. For awhile, she was known as the "Mysterious Colorado Woman," her name is Katrina Perry. Her work is known and much admired here in Washington, D.C. and I had wished to include it in the book. Katrina, if you're out there, I would love to hear from you.

I would like to thank Mr. Mike Solos of Polyform Products Co. for his invaluable editing of the plastics chemistry chapter. This is an important part of the book and I am very grateful to him for his time and input. Dr. William Bailey, professor of chemistry at the University of Maryland, was also a great help at the outset of my research in reviewing with me the information I had obtained. I would also like to thank Helmut Gerber of Eberhard Faber for his review of the plastics chapter and valuable amendments and additions.

I would like to thank Penny and Eric Diamanti de Widt for their continual support of all my efforts in the last two years. They have acted as gatherers and disseminators of information on artists and have played a very active role in promoting the work of polymer clay artists through their shop "Beadazzled," in Washington, DC. In many ways I owe this book to them. Thank you both.

I would also like to thank Anita Roberts, my boss, who endured this year and a half with sometimes half an employee, and has supported and encouraged me throughout. She has also made it possible for me to learn more about computers, without which the writing would have been grueling.

Last but not least, I want to thank my husband, John, who has endured a year and a half of no vacations and my mental and emotional absence for much of the rest of the time. He has been my supporter and helper, editor, cook, housekeeper, telephone answering service, and most of all, my companion and friend. I could not have done it without him.

Finally, I want to thank all of my students. They have been the source of so many ideas and inspirations and so much enthusiasm that it kept me going when I got bogged down. They have waited patiently for this book. I hope it will not disappoint them.

Nan Roche
College Park, MD   November, 1990

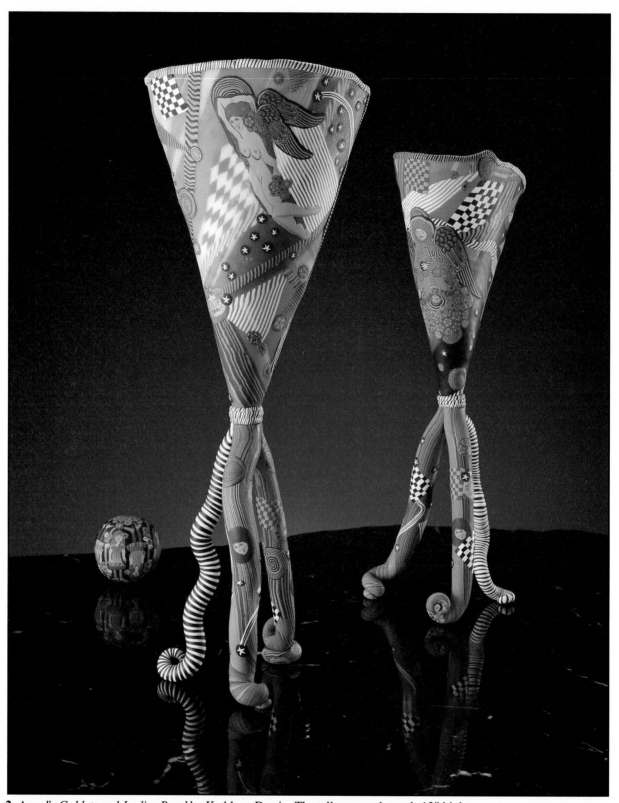

2. *Angel's Goblets* and *Ladies Bead* by Kathleen Dustin. The tallest vessel stands 12" high.

Foreword

While attending the American University of Beirut in 1971, a Lebanese friend gave me a key ring as a memento of our friendship. Attached to it he'd made a small brown disc bearing a simple yellow design. As I examined it, I was intrigued by the material. It was somewhat flexible and I could see that the yellow decoration had been pressed into the brown background rather than painted on. When I asked him what material it was, he told me he'd gotten this colored, hobby, modeling clay in West Germany, that it was easy to work just with one's fingers, and that it had been baked in an ordinary oven to make it permanent.

Although I didn't remember the brand name at the time, it was my first introduction to the polymer clay product called Fimo. Little did I dream that almost 20 years later the use of polymer clay would be an artistic focal point for me. In the early 1980's I chanced upon a selection of colored Fimo bars while traveling through Austria. I recognized it as the material that must have been used in my key ring memento. With no particular purpose in mind, I bought some of the Fimo and within two years had produced a series of twenty soft- sculpture female figures whose hands, feet and faces had been sculpted from polymer clay.

Back in the United States, I became acquainted with Sculpey III, the American colored polymer-clay product. Because ceramic sculpture and jewelry had been my primary pursuits, however, I utilized Fimo and Sculpey III only sporadically, and in a limited fashion. That phase lasted until a friend showed me a necklace of multi-colored beads made by Pier Voulkos, whose work appears in this book. My friend didn't know what the beads were made of, but again I recognized the material as Fimo, and also recognized that the technique used to achieve the colored patterns was essentially the same as that used to make the simple brown and yellow key ring. Immediately the artistic potential struck me for using inlaid color, rather than painted-on surface decoration to make all kinds of jewelry, and even other art forms.

So began for me what has been a compelling exploration of using the colors in these materials, to achieve designs and decoration by inlaying color, twisting color, and manipulating color in millefiore. Apart from some inspiration from Jane Peiser's work in ceramics, simply working with polymer clay, experimenting and pushing it to its limits, led me into these techiques because of its capacity to execute them easily and quickly.

Obviously I was not the only craftsman seized by these ideas because while I was developing effective polymer clay techniques, others were doing the same, independently. Gradually, a quiet but talented artistic movement, enthusiastically dedicated to polymer clay, has emerged in the past few years. Now, for the first time, our collective knowledge concerning this new medium has been compiled in a book. While the techniques and information presented here are as comprehensive as possible at this time, artistic and technical horizons will expand as enthusiasm and respect for polymer clay continue to spread.

This book is an important introduction to a remarkable material. While polymer clay is not a traditional craft medium that has been "proven" through the ages, many of the techniques presented here are traditional. Borrowed from other media, they have been easily adapted for use with a contemporary material. Artists, craftsmen and connoisseurs should not take polymer clay lightly because of its comparative youth. The artistic vision, and the quality of the craftsmanship should determine its validity.

I have found that an amazing characteristic of polymer clay is its dynamism - its capacity for infinite variety. Visual and textural surfaces, working techniques, compatibility with other media, and function are all elements which invite further exploration.

Here also, Nan Roche gives us a taste of other polymer clay applications besides jewelry, which, because of my training, have always held a tremendous attraction for me: sculpture, vessel forms, and objects. Nan Roche has worked hard on this book with the help of many others, but the future will undoubtedly show it only to have scratched the surface of the subject. I know we can look forward to continued aesthetic growth in the use of polymer clay, as well as to concept- provoking refinements in its technical characteristics.

When I look at it today, my simple key ring represents possibilities that still appear unlimited. And I find that very exciting.

Kathleen Dustin, M.F.A.
Ankara, Turkey

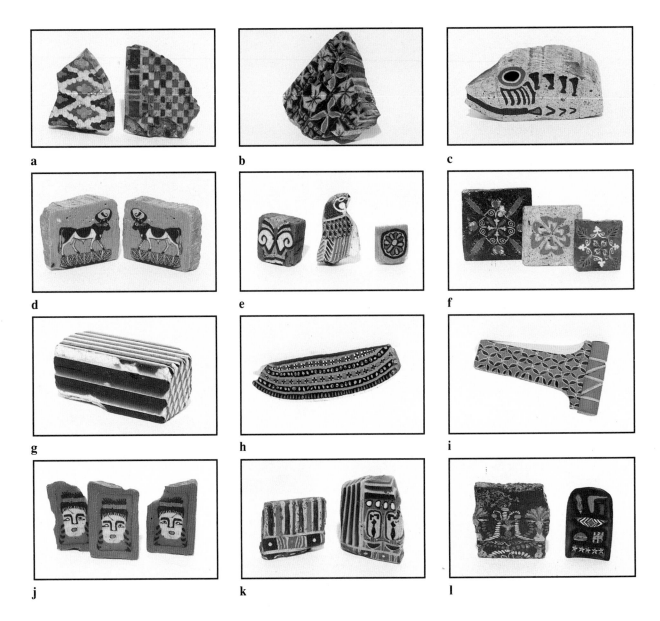

3. Fused Mosaic Plaques, Egypt, from the 1st Century B.C. to the 1st Century A.D. Courtesy of the Smithsonian Institution, Freer Gallery of Art, Washington, DC. Photographed by Marty Amt.
a. Two mosaic fragments. Accession nos. 09.604, 09.605. Height: 1", 1 1/8".
b. Rosette fragment. Accession no.: 09.512. Height 1".
c. Fishhead cane. Accession no.: 09.? 1" x 2".
d. Double bull slice. Accession no.: 09.530. 1 3/8" x 1 1/2".
e. Three misc. tiles. Accession nos.: 09.482, 09.506, 09.467. 1/2", 3/4", 3/8".
f. Three rosettes. Accession nos.: 09.470, 09.469, 09.467. 1", 3/4" 5/8".
g. Purple/white cane. Accession no.: 09.528. 1" x 2".
h. Long border tile. Accession no.: 09.460. 1/2" x 2 1/4".
i. Red hieroglyph. Accession no.: 09.461. 1 7/8" x 1".
j. Female face, three slices. Accession no.: 09.496. 1".
k. Two fragments. Accession nos.: 09.499, 09.502. 3/4"x 1 1/8".
l. Two small tiles. Accession nos.: 09.523, 09.500. 5/8", 5/8".

Introduction

So what is this "new clay" and why learn about it? It is plastic, not really new, and not a clay. "Plastic" has been a loaded word in our modern world, associated with words like "cheap" and "throwaway". But, this "new clay" is plastic in the BEST sense of the word. It will do most of the things that traditional materials like, ceramics, wood and glass, will do, and much more besides, but with fewer tools and no apprenticeship. It is one of the most versatile and inspirational artist's materials to come along in centuries.

You may have come across the new clay in art stores or toy stores under the brand names "Sculpey" or "Fimo." It has been around for about 30 years, so I call it "new" only in the context of more traditional art materials, like porcelain and glass. It has been used by doll makers, miniaturists, architects and children for about that long, but now is being used in exciting and innovative ways by artists and craftsman around the world. This attention has come along with a resurgence of interest in the crafts, particularly wearable art and jewelry. Wearing art is a statement of your personal aesthetic, whether you are the artist, or someone else has captured a mood for you. Expression is what we're after and the new clay is ripe with possibilities.

This material is accessible to everyone. It requires very little equipment and is easy to work with. Best of all there are no preconceived notions about the "right" way to use it. There are no mistakes. Every effort seems to yield new possibilities. It is very freeing. You can do almost anything with it.

Because it is so accessible and so full of possibilities, it sparks your sense of play, experimentation and curiosity. That is where your art is. Art is something we all have in us. Unfortunately in our culture, it is often put away with our childhood toys. But art is not separable from us. It is an innate property of being human, like eating, sleeping and dreaming. Older tribal peoples around the world, like the Hmong, the Latvians, and the Balinese, do not separate art from the common person and the people in these cultures are allowed to express themselves artistically, without judgement. Even simple functional items are decorated with designs of personal significance. Art seems to bubble up naturally when given the chance.

So let the doors open. Embrace your childhood and that wonderful, free, non-judgmental sense of play. Do you remember it? This material will help you find it again. Look around you for inspiration. Our world is so rich with stimuli it is often overwhelming. Both the natural world of water, sky and flowers, and the man made world of buildings, electronics and fabrics are rich sources of ideas. Even things that are mundane - cracks in the sidewalk and drops of water on a leaf - are all there to notice and interpret. To me the world is a visual banquet for perpetual tasting, but I never get full.

When you look twice at something in the world, why do you? Is it the color, the form, or the emotional content of the object that you like? Pay attention to what catches your eye. Try imitation. The stimuli in your everyday life is a fertile source of inspiration. Television takes us all over the world, and museums and books take us into the past. We are rapidly becoming global people with the beauty and diversity of all the world's cultures available from which to learn. The way in which you integrate the world outside you with your own personal experiences, will emerge in your play with the clay. So leave aside the adult world of judgement, work and limitations, and come on a journey of discovery with this wonderful new clay. No experience necessary.

The Aim of This Book

There is a desperate need to present working methods and information about the polymer clays. A few small pamphlets exist, produced by the manufacturers, but the scope of this book will be to present the polymer clays as a new art medium deserving of serious attention. The book will attempt to do two things: to consolidate the information available about the different products and present a broad range of possible working techniques to stimulate your imagination; and to present contemporary artworks to illustrate what is possible.

A lot of people around the country are already quietly discovering what this material, this **new clay**, can do. Artists rooted in more traditional art media are translating their skills and knowledge into working with this modern material. As you will see, the versatility of this new material is unique in that it will allow translation of techniques from almost every craft tradition. The artists represented in this book come from many different disciplines: ceramics, glass, metals, jewelry design with beads and elements, bookmaking, textiles, sculpture and collage. Some of them have other artistic interests in theater, music, literature and science, and their work often reflects these multiple talents. However, you need not have any particular skill or knowledge to work with this clay. I hope to bring to you many of these ideas and techniques with simplicity and clarity.

First will be a discussion of the basic properties and characteristics of the clay followed by chapters on tools and color mixing. Clay preparation leads into a chapter covering the basic shapes - the ball, the log or snake, and the sheet. Then follows a section presenting techniques that use these shapes, with drawings and photos illustrating each one. Complex canes and loaves are discussed next as a logical extension of the preceding techniques. Chapters on surface treatments, collage and sculpture, including dolls and vessels, are followed with a mention of other ways in which the clay may be used, including buttons, books and wall pieces. The appendices include a bibliography, a glossary of terms, a listing of the artists represented and a list of suppliers. Finally, there is an appendix on plastics chemistry for those of you who want to understand more.

I hope this book will be useful to the beginner as well as to those more advanced. By progressing from the simplest to the more complex techniques, you should be able to build upon your knowledge with each step. There are so many different modes of working with the clay that there is a lifetime of techniques to explore. You can return time and time again to different portions of the book for inspiration and ideas. You will most certainly discover many ideas on your own.

The more advanced user will find many methods of working with the clay that may be combined with his or her own current repertoire of techniques. Artists working in other media may be able to bring concepts and techniques from their media and apply it to this material. I hope that artists from many different disciplines will seriously consider what the new clay has to offer.

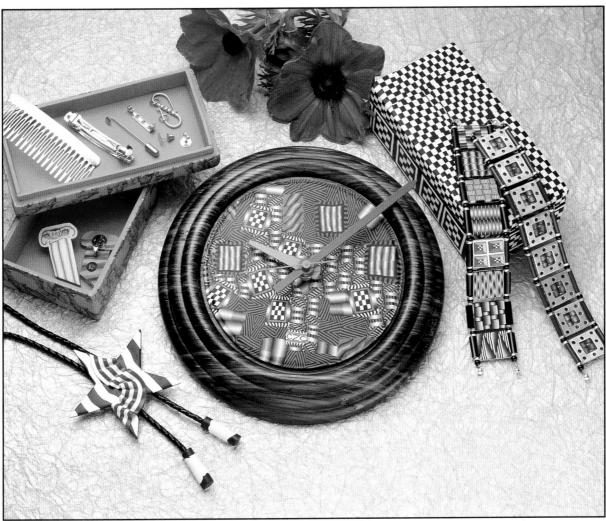

4. Findings. On the left of the photo is a box by **Grove and Grove**, with a collection of findings in the top and a pair of earrings titled *Doric Columns with Angels*, by Kathleen Amt. Below is a bolo tie by **Grove and Grove**. The clock is by **City Zen Cane**. To the right is a box by **Grove and Grove** with two bracelets by **City Zen Cane**, showing the front and back surfaces. **City Zen Cane** had the elements of the bracelets made to their specifications. The boxes are made of slabs and are constructed of Fimo.

Background

I have collected beads for as long as I can remember. As a small child I collected brightly colored seeds and colored pieces of glass as well. These objects were like jewels and treasures and possessed other-worldly powers in my imagination. They still do, and not only to me: beads have a universal appeal that extends backward in time to early human habitations over 40,000 years ago.[1] Although I have collected beads from all over the world, the most fascinating and beautiful of these were made of glass in 19th century Venice for trade around the world, particularly to Africa. Some of these African trade beads, called **millefiori** or "thousand flowers," are beautifully decorated with flowers or geometric designs. Though each one is hand made and unique, they are so beautiful and precious that it is hard to imagine <u>how</u> they were made. My quest for the answer has led me, eventually, to my encounter with polymer clay.

Living in Washington, DC, with all of its wonderful national museums, I first encountered the antecedent to these marvelous Venetian beads, in the Freer Gallery of Art. These very rare, ancient, Roman face and figure mosaic glass canes were made between the 2nd century BC and 2nd century AD. These are some of the most exquisite objects ever made in glass. I was determined to find out all I could about how they were made.

It was not easy. The details of their manufacture had been all but lost. There are several glass artists who are now interested in trying to recreate these ancient techniques. I went to Penland School of design in North Carolina to learn lampworking in glass from Paul Stankard, hoping this would yield clues. Lampworking is the method used to produce many of the Venetian beads by melting colored rods of glass in front of a flame and applying the molten glass to a bead. The colors can be trailed or wound onto the surface or dotted for eye beads. But lampworking techniques alone could not reproduce these ancient, glass mosaic pieces. Moreover, none of the other glassworkers at Penland were certain about how they were made, either.

It was not until I encountered Kathleen Dustin and my first workshop on bead making with polymer clay that things were clarified. As she began to illustrate the wonderful properties of the clay, I became more and more excited. I realized that it could do what few other materials could - mimic the processes of the ancient glassworkers. Though the actual processes of working with molten glass to produce these pieces still remains a mystery, at least the concepts of building an image in a cane or loaf are clearly illustrated by working with this clay.

Caneworking - making a image that runs through a loaf - is one of the techniques most easily done with this clay. There are few other materials that possess the properties needed to do this; namely, maintaining separation of colors while being stretched or reduced in size. In addition to glass, many people have worked with colored porcelains[2] and colored wax using caneworking techniques. Candy making is another application you may have encountered, with the colorful holiday candies being most common. But each of these materials require special equipment and technical skills and do not possess the wide range of colors nor the easy accessibility of the polymer clays.

a

b

c

d

e

5. Fused Mosaic Plaques, Egypt, from the 1st Century B.C. to the 1st Century A.D. Courtesy of the Smithsonian Institution, Freer Gallery of Art, Washington, DC. Photographed by Marty Amt.
a. Three half-face tiles. Accession numbers: 09.487, 09.490, 09.486. Height: 1 1/2", 1 1/4", 1 1/4".
b. Double satyr face. Accession no. 09.529. 1 1/4".
c. Satyr face cane. Accession no. 09.529. 1 1/4" x 2 1/2".
d. Three goddess tiles. Accession nos.: 09.488, 09.493, 09.489. Height: 1 1/4", 1", 1 1/2".
e. Three face tiles. Accession nos.: 09.511, 09.493, 09.491. Height: 5/8", 1", 7/8".

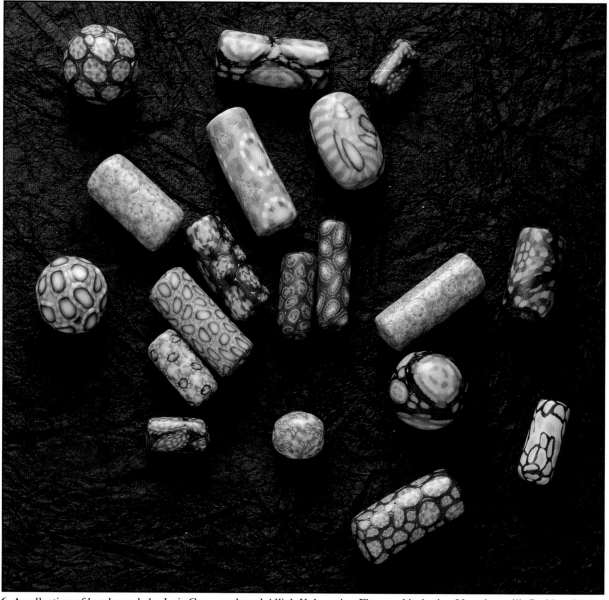

6. A collection of beads made by Lois Grommesh and Alliah Kahn using Fimo and imitating Venetian millefiori beads.

The Basics

The new clay is really an old friend. It is a plastic called polyvinyl chloride, something we use in our lives every day. It is soft and moldable at room temperature and is hardened and fused into a permanent plastic with heat. It comes in wonderful colors, won't shrink, and does things no other material on earth will do. It is definitely not a natural material but it can be made to look like one. It can be carved, stamped, drilled, and painted. It can be used to make molds. In thin sheets it can be draped like cloth. It can imitate wood, metal, stone, and fabric. It is one of the most exciting art and jewelry making materials to come along in years.

People have worked with traditional clay for thousands of years. It is probably one of the earliest materials that mankind employed to make objects for utilitarian use, and ornamentation. To me, the act of working with clay sparks an ancient resonance with the past, and this new material is no less inspiring than the ancient one.

Strictly speaking, of course, it is _not_ clay. Clay consists of hydrated silicates of aluminum or, in other words, finely ground sand particles mixed with water. Porcelains, which are made from a very fine white clay, called kaolin, and other earthen clays require very high temperatures to melt and fuse the silicates together. Glass too, is a silicate, and the realms of glass and clay come together in fundamental and interesting ways. Glass is composed of silicates mixed with soda and lime which are also fused at high temperatures. In many ways the development of glass arose from ceramics technology. The earliest precursor of glass, called faience, was made in Egypt around 4000 BC. It is similar to glazed ceramics, and represents a transition technology between ceramics and glass.[3]

The polymer clays have a great deal in common conceptually with these two traditional materials even though they are composed of fundamentally different substances. The new clay is similar because it is composed of microscopic particles of polyvinyl chloride in suspension with a plasticizer that allows it to be modeled like clay. Heat applied to these particles fuses them, much the same way that firing clay fuses the silicates into a hardened durable product.

Finally the question of what to call this new clay must be considered. Though it is not a clay, it does behave like clay in all of the essential ways. The most accurate choice would be to call it polymer clay, because it is made up of vinyl chloride polymer in suspension. But polymer clay is a cumbersome and technical term that may be intimidating. Many people refer to it by the various brand names like Sculpey or Fimo. But, I find these names unappealing and the different brands are basically the same chemically, though each is compounded differently and have slightly different properties. Rather than referring to specific brands by name throughout the book, I will call this "new clay" simply "clay," prefacing it with the words "new" or "polymer" where appropriate to the discussion. This is with the understanding that the word clay is being used in the broadest possible sense of the word, and is descriptive only.

The Basics

Though it looks and feels like clay, there are many wonderful properties of polymer clay that are quite different from any other art material. It can be used like clay, but it will also fold and drape like fabric. It can be stamped and textured like metal. It can be sawed, sanded and drilled like wood. It can be painted and used in collage and three-dimensional sculpture.

The new clay contains no water and is not mixable with water. It will not dry out, even when stored exposed on your work bench. When baked for 20 minutes at a moderate temperature of $270^{\circ}F$, the clay fuses into a hard durable plastic.

The separation of colors is maintained even when the clay is squeezed into a smaller size. About the only other material that acts in this manner is molten glass, which is considerably more difficult to work with! This property has all sorts of marvelous consequences. For example, you can make a design by layering clay colors and reduce the size by pressing, retaining the exact image. You will see works in this book that use this property with great imagination by repeating the same design element in different sizes and shapes. This property also makes polymer clay uniquely suited to imitation of the Roman glass mosaics and millefiori canes mentioned in the introduction.

Another wonderful property of the new clay is its lack of shrinkage during baking. This allows you to include collage materials and findings during baking without risking distortion. (You will have to be sure, of course, that the collage materials themselves can withstand the baking temperatures.) Anyone who has worked with ceramics, where there is considerable shrinkage during firing, will appreciate this. What you see is what you get with this clay.

Different Brands

There are four available brands of polymer clay - Sculpey, Fimo, Cernit and Modello. Though they are chemically similar and can be used together, they each have slightly different properties and hardening temperatures. There may be other brands available, but they have not yet been imported into the US. [See the suppliers listing in the appendix.] Sculpey is the only American brand. The company, Polyform Products in Illinois, has been in existence for about 30 years. They make a range of types of clay and have recently come out with some new products. Colored Sculpey III is the best of their products. It comes in 30 colors, some of which are metallic and pearlescent, as well as a translucent clay. It is the softest of the brands, and does not require a lot of kneading. For this reason it is my favorite. It does not have the same tensile strength as some of the other brands, however. Many artists use combinations of the different brands for various purposes.

The other products are also noteworthy because they have particular properties that you will find useful. You may be familiar with the original white Sculpey from grade-school art class. Super Sculpey is the next development and is slightly more durable, but comes only in a tan color. Many people mix this product with Fimo to give it strength or to increase Fimo's softness, or it may be mixed with colored Sculpey III. The company has recently developed a new, stronger clay called Promat, which is a little more difficult to knead, resembling Fimo. It also sells an elastic clay that

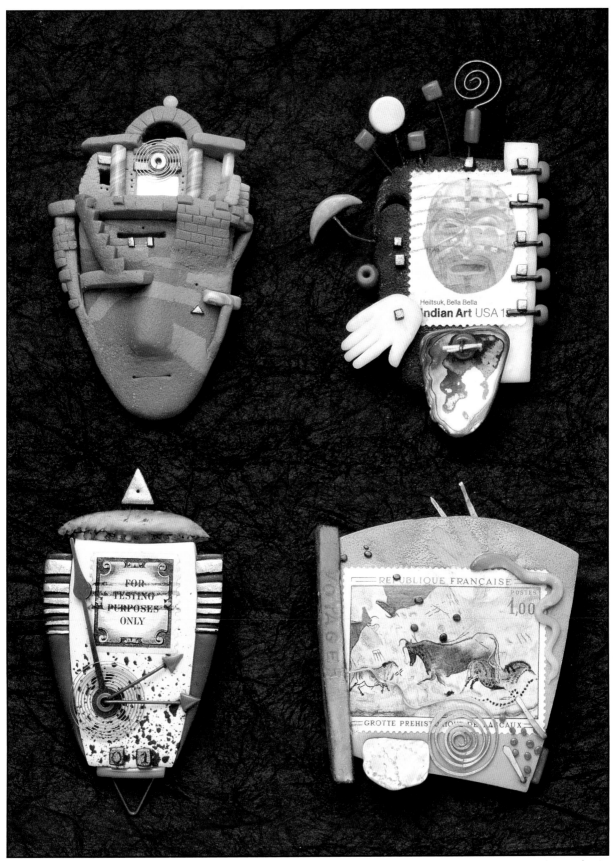

7. Four pins by Tory Hughes. Tory uses stamps and other collage materials combined with mythic symbols to refer to events in time and place.

retains its elasticity after baking, and a liquid Sculpey for mold making. Sculpey is very opaque and develops a nice patina when baked. To my eye, it looks the least like plastic.

Fimo is a German product, made by the Eberhard-Faber Company. It comes in 39 colors including a translucent and a glow-in-the-dark color, and may be the easiest to find in many locations. Fimo is very stiff when it comes out of the package and requires more kneading than Sculpey, but is stronger. Once the clay has been kneaded or conditioned, it remains smooth and workable for a long time. There are numerous strategies for softening and kneading which I will discuss in the next section. Eberhard-Faber makes two lacquers which are excellent, a matte and a glossy. They also publish a series of pamphlets which are nicely done.

Cernit is another German product made by the T+F GmbH Company. It is imported by Handcraft Designs in Hatfield, PA. Cernit now comes in 37 colors, including 12 pearlescent and 6 neon colors. It has a porcelain-like finish and is the most translucent of the various brands. Many doll makers prefer this product because it most closely resembles the translucency of skin. It has the highest tensile strength of them all. The stiffness and workability is somewhere between Sculpey and Fimo.

Modello is the least commonly found of the clays. It is very opaque and fairly soft, like Sculpey. It is made by the Reiser Company in Nurenberg, Germany.

Each of the brands of polymer clay comes in its own color palette. They may be freely combined with one another. With iridescent, pearlescent, metallic, neon, translucent colors and even glow-in-dark colors, the possibilities are infinite. The colors can be used unmixed, but one of the wonderful things about this clay is that you can mix your own palette very easily, just by kneading wads of the clay together. You will notice, when you do, that a beautiful swirl of the two colors will develop before complete mixing. If you use natural colors, the effect will be reminiscent of marble or agate. If you continue to knead, the clay will mix into one solid color. More about color mixing and the color wheel will be discussed later.

Safety Notes

For many artists today, there is a greater awareness of the toxicity of the materials they use. It has become an important topic because artists tend to use their materials heavily and continuously over a long period of time. This is why potential problems can arise.

These clays are not toxic for ordinary use. Those of you who will be casual users - working just a few hours a week with it - need not worry. I want to express some caution, however, for heavy users of the polymer clays.

A potential hazard arises from the plasticizer that is used to make the clay malleable. You may notice that when the clay is removed from its wrapper and placed on a piece of paper, an oily ring develops. This is caused by residual plasticizer leaching out of the unbaked clay. For this reason the clay should not be worked in the vicinity of food or food preparation tools or surfaces. Always bake your clay in a well-ventilated work area. At temperatures above what is recommended, the clay may emit noxious fumes. Once the clay has been baked and hardened, it becomes essentially inert and should be considered non-toxic for ordinary use.

I would add a word of caution about making objects from the clay that might be used for holding foods. This clay, and many other plastics, are porous and may have some amount of residual plasticizer left, even after hardening, that could be released by acidic foods or liquids (Tupperware-type plastics are in the safe category). For this reason, do not use tools or surfaces which might come in contact with foods, and wash your hands carefully after working with the clay.

These cautions are best understood in light of the manufacture and chemistry of this plastic, so if you want a more thorough explanation, refer to the section on plastics chemistry in the back of the book.

I want to stress that only those of you who will be working with the clay daily need have any concern. As a compromise, I tend to use plastic surgical gloves when doing a lot of mixing and kneading of the clay, and leave my hands bare when doing detail work. Remember that many artists' materials - paints, dyes, potters' glazes, and photographic chemicals - present hazards to individuals when heavily used and not respected. There is no need to be overly paranoid, just prudently cautious.

Storage

Though the new clay will not dry out with time, its real enemies are prolonged exposure to heat and ultraviolet light. Heat will slowly fuse the clay and make it brittle and crumbly until it is totally unworkable. To avoid this, store your clay in a cool dark place and plan to use it within a year from purchase. Ultraviolet light is the other enemy and produces much the same effect as the prolonged heat. Do not place the raw clay, or pieces that have been baked, in a sunny window for long periods of time.

Raw clay and unbaked work should not be allowed to remain in contact with most other plastics. Many other plastics are also porous and will soak up the residual plasticizer and become softened by it, with the unfortunate effect of having your clay stick permanently to it. To avoid this problem, I use wax paper which is non-reactive to the raw polymer. Other people use plastic wrap and plastic sandwich bags, which also seem to be inert, for clay storage. Not all plastic wrap is the same, so be sure to test it before you use it. Over time, even when protected by these products, the plasticizer will still leach through and can cause problems, so check your stored clay from time to time. I use plastic storage containers lined with wax paper, and store my raw clay in kneaded, flattened pillow shapes between layers of wax paper. Unbaked clay is a magnet for dust particles, hair and fibers, so some consideration should be given to protecting your work.

Baking

Baking is one of the most important factors to understand when working with the polymer clays. Frequently, people purchase the clay, make something wonderful from it and promptly BURN it to a crisp. Reading the label on the package won't necessarily help. The label tells you the average baking temperature and time to use, but there is other information that you need for success.

First, let's discuss baking temperatures. Each brand of clay lists an optimum temperature for its product. These temperatures range from $212^{o}F$ - $300^{o}F$, depending on the brand and color. The range of temperatures is probably due to differences in the types of additives. Fimo lists $212^{o}F$ for some of the transparent and flesh-tone colors, $265^{o}F$ for black, and $275^{o}F$ for most other colors. Cernit gives a range of $215 - 270^{o}F$ and Sculpey lists all of its colors at $300^{o}F$. Does it seem confusing? Don't worry, we will be able to make sense out of it. The polyvinyl chloride grains that make up the clay, have to melt together with heat to produce a hard plastic. If the temperature is too low, you get incomplete fusion and a soft or crumbly product; if it is too high, the PVC is fused (and burnt) on the outside before the heat reaches the inside. The idea is to get a constant, even, permeating heat throughout the clay for proper fusion.

Most of us run into problems with our ovens, whether using a large oven or toaster oven. Often the temperature setting on the dial does not accurately reflect the temperature in the oven. Both toaster ovens and large ovens go through a temperature range as they cycle on and off, attempting to maintain a stable temperature. The range can be from 5 to 15 degrees. This will vary depending on the sensitivity of the oven thermostat. It is important to get a good oven thermometer and check the temperature throughout several heating cycles. Try to shoot for around 270°F. Mark this setting on the dial and set your oven here every time you bake.

You should bake your clay away from the heating elements where the temperature may be locally hotter than the thermometer indicates. Use a non- conducting surface to bake on, such as slate, a ceramic plate or a pyrex baking dish. One manufacturer recommends baking on a thick, tempered glass plate. This will help moderate the heat. Pre-heat your oven with the baking surface inside. Everyone will need to experiment a little bit with his or her own baking setup. At first, bake some items that aren't important until you are satisfied with the results.

As for baking times, the manufacturers recommend anything from 5 minutes to 30 minutes. If you think about it, the size of the object will have a lot to do with it. For a small object, the heat will soak through quickly and it will be fused in a short time, larger objects will need more time.

Consider what happens when the temperature is too hot: the small object will be heated and fused very rapidly and then proceed to burn; the larger one will have to be baked longer and may burn on the outside before it gets fused on the inside. For this reason, most people use lower baking temperatures and bake for longer periods of time. Some of the manufacturers' labels are very misleading: 300°F for 20 minutes in an inaccurate home oven is a recipe for failure. Use 260 - 270°F for 30 minutes or longer for better results. Be sure to use the lower temperature (212°) for Fimo transparent and flesh colors. When these colors are used with other colors and do not predominate you may use the higher temperature. You must wait until your work is completely cool to test for "doneness". Once cool, the piece will be completely hard and make a sharp sound when rapped on the table. If it is not completely done it will feel like a firm grapefruit and "give" a little to pressure. Don't go too low on the heat - you must have enough heat to get complete fusion of the PVC grains into a single mass.

As mentioned before, when baking the clay you will notice a plastic smell coming out of your oven. Make sure you have adequate ventilation when you are baking. If you are baking daily - you should have an additional fan driven exhaust vent attached to your oven. The burned clay is not healthy to breathe and burning should be avoided. If you burn a batch of clay, turn off your oven and take the burned clay outside, being careful not to breathe the fumes. If an accident happens, ventilate the room thoroughly. After baking, the plastic is essentially inert, but I would never use anything made out of the clay for direct contact with food. Infants and pets, especially birds, should not be left in an unventilated room with baking clay.

Most polymer clays will not change color if baked for the proper amount of time. The darker colors of Fimo, like navy blue, violet and terra cotta will get darker. Sculpey has a matte patina on the surface after baking, whereas Fimo and Cernit remain smoother. Over-baking burns the polymer clay much like burnt cookies and the colors darken. Transparent and white are especially susceptible to burning. If your pieces contain a lot of white, use a lower temperature.

8. Kimono wallpiece by Abby Rohrer. Dimensions are about 5" by 8".

9. The work place, showing beads on a baking tray and a pasta machine with clay being rolled through it. The clay has a piece of gold leaf on the surface which fractures as it goes through the pasta machine. In the background is a pin by Kaz Yamashita using this technique and next to it a pin by Nan Roche. Notice the cane in the foreground with slices cut, packages of Cernit, Fimo, and Sculpey, a slicing blade and needle tool and a piece of gold leafing.

Tools

The process of finding and making tools for working with polymer clay is a basic part of your own artistic expression. The tools and materials themselves will often determine your discoveries and inventions. There is a tremendous thrill associated with finding a new tool that generates new ideas.

Hands

Your hands are one of the most complex and versatile tools you could possible need. You must learn to use them just as you would any other tool. Everyone's hands are a different shape and size, and this will make a difference. Be patient with yourself and find your own working style. For many of you, your hands may be the only tools you will ever want to use. Take a look at them now. Notice the shape of the palms and how complex a shape they really are. Each hand may be slightly different in size, depending on whether you are right or left handed, due to muscle development. How deep are the cups of your hands? Where are the smooth parts and where are the bumpy parts. When you roll clay, those shapes will be reflected in the clay. To roll a very even and smooth log of clay you will need to know what part of your hand to use.

When working with the clay, you will find that some of it sticks to your hands. It is helpful to keep a rough cloth nearby to wipe your hands, especially when working with several colors. Be sure to work with white and pastel colors first as the darker colors, like red and blue, will rub off and contaminate the lighter colors. Because polymer clay is not mixable with water, washing your hands will not completely remove it. Ordinary rubbing alcohol will work but dries out your hands. The best thing to use is a good quality hand cream and then a coarse towel. Any residual clay color can then be removed by washing.

Surfaces

The ideal working surface is one to which the clay will not stick, is smooth, and will not move around when you are working on it. For portability and cost, wax paper is the easiest to use and can be taped onto a table or counter. Make sure it is smooth and taut and well taped before trying to work on it. Another excellent surface is high-density polyurethane or lucite plastic, either clear or opaque. I prefer a white, opaque working surface to see my work better. Plastics like lucite and plexiglas can be obtained from a good hardware store or plastics specialty store. Check your yellow pages. Sometimes a leather working supply store will carry a variety of plastics and other surfaces on which to punch and work leather. If the plastic is textured your work will be textured as well, so check for scratches and marks before buying. Texture is not necessarily an undesirable characteristic. With texture in mind, you may wish to shop for plastic or other materials to add to your collection of texturing "tools". A thick glass plate with beveled edges or a smooth marble slab also make excellent working surfaces. An old piece of Formica counter top will also work well.

Cutting Tools

Cutting tools are very important. The clay can be cut like a roll of cookies or thin slices may be shaved off a larger, more complex loaf. In order to make thin slices with reasonable success you need the best possible blade. A single edged razor blade will do, but it is thicker than I like to use and it doesn't have a long blade length. You will see why the blade length is important later on. A better blade can be obtained at the hardware or paint supply store. Look for wallpaper scraper blades; there are many varieties of these but look for the thinnest and longest you can find. You may want to put a piece of masking tape along the blunt edge of the blade to avoid cutting yourself with the sharp edge. The very best of blades are surgical microtome blades used by pathologists to make ultrathin sections of tissues for study. They are very long and thin but very strong and made of stainless steel. Some of the scientific supply companies may carry them. [See the suppliers listing in the appendix.] Of course, if you are not making thin slices from canes, an ordinary paring knife or Exacto knife will do just fine.

Piercing Tools

The simplest of piercing tools are to be found in your sewing box - needles. They come in all lengths and thicknesses, with blunt and sharp ends. You will be piercing your clay when making beads and ornaments that will be hung on necklaces. Other materials, like shell, glass or stones are very difficult to drill, requiring specialized tools and drill bits. The wonderful thing about polymer clay is that it can be pierced in many different ways very easily, before baking. You can now depart from the limitations of "ordinary" linear strings of beads and make spacing beads and divider bars with multiple perforations. When thinking about making beads, attention should be paid to the thread onto which the beads will be strung. Your holes should be just small enough to contain the thread and hold the beads snugly. For this reason a selection of needles or boring tools will be useful to have around. They will be easier to use if they are reasonably long. A sharp or blunt point may be used.

A wonderful little tool that will make your piercing infinitely easier is a pin vise. This is a gripping device designed to close around the end of a small object and hold it firmly, much the same way a drill closes around a drill bit. If your budget is limited, however, you do not need to buy any special tools. Maureen Carlson makes her own pin holders and shaping tools out of the clay itself. To do this, form a handle out of clay and press the needle into one end. The other end of the handle may be shaped into a point, wedge, or left blunt for many possible uses. Then bake it.

Shaping Tools

Shaping tools can be made out of clay and baked or found around the house. The handles of artists' paintbrushes make wonderful blunt shaping tools. Wooden ceramic tools can also be found in art supply stores. Another clever tool that Maureen Carlson recommends is a paintbrush with a small amount of clay worked into the bristles. Use it as a smoothing tool for the surface of unbaked clay. The clay worked into the bristles gives just enough body to the brush to do the job nicely.

Texturing Tools

Texturing can be achieved in many ways. You will need to keep your eyes open for tools and objects that will make a texture. Experiment with different surfaces. One simple chisel like tool can be used to make many different textures. Hardware stores are great sources for texturing materials. Another good source of texturing tools is your dentist's office. Often dentists have old worn tools that they would be happy to give to you. You may be on a waiting list however - other patients may be artists and have the same idea. New dental tools can often be found in some of the mail order tool and woodworking catalogs.

Leather punches are wonderful texturing tools. These can be found at Tandy Leather Stores and other leather work suppliers. Keep on the look out at garage sales, flea markets, antique fairs and auctions for old tools. Sometimes old leather working tools and other tools with potential will turn up. Remember, finding that special tool can be a major ingredient in your art work, and is a part of the whole process of making art. It is also part of the fun.

Found Materials

All kinds of found materials can be used as texturing devices. Polymer clay can be pressed onto baskets and cloth to produce texture. Old grainy wood will give a wood-like texture. Leaves, seeds, berries and barks that have interesting texture can be used like stamps on the clay. Plastic netting, the design on the back of your favorite silverware or a special spoon that you found at a garage sale, old pieces of costume jewelry, combs, brocade fabrics and cookie molds are all full of potential. Once you start experimenting, you'll tear your house apart with glee looking for things

10. Three pins by Ann Kahn made with Fimo. The size is 1 1/4 inches square. Notice how effective and expressive a simple scored line can be as a design.

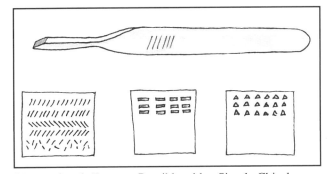

Illustration 1. Textures Possible with a Simple Chisel.

to use. Don't worry, it's perfectly natural. After all, you didn't really want to grow up, did you? I tend to make small samples of textures, that are especially interesting, to keep for future reference. It's a good idea to do this with all the techniques that will be taught in this book. Often you will forget about a certain wonderful idea and these test pieces, when baked, are an excellent reminder.

Rolling Tools

Many of the techniques that will be described in more detail later will use flat sheets of polymer clay. There are several different ways to get a flat sheet of clay: you may use a rolling pin, a printer's brayer, your hands, a pasta machine or a straight drinking glass.

The rolling pin is the obvious choice for flattening clay. The standard wooden pin is not really ideal, however: the wood grain will leave an impression on the clay and the clay is likely to stick to it. A marble or stone pastry rolling pin is much better. These can be found at a specialty cooking supply stores.

A printer's brayer is another excellent flattening tool. It is a roller attached to a handle that is used to spread ink onto printing blocks. These are made from many different materials: wood, plastic and rubber, depending on what kind of ink it is designed to work with. Again the wood and rubber varieties may leave a texture on the polymer clay. The best type of brayer to use is the clear acrylic type, though they are sometimes hard to find. The

11. A pin and a pair of earrings by Karen Hubert. Notice the use of texture, shape and metallic thread in the design. The patterned elements are made from a cane.

brayer will end up being one of your most-used tools. You will use it when joining two pieces of clay, or stacking sheets of color for mosaic work, or squaring off a round roll of clay for square elements. Look for different types of brayers at art supply stores and paint stores or in the wallpapering and drywalling section of the hardware store.

The pasta machine is incomparable to any other tool in the polymer clay workshop. You can get along without it, but it will allow so much more precision and ease that it is a highly recommended investment. You may requisition your old kitchen model, but do not go back to using it for food - it will be nearly impossible to remove all the residual polymer clay. If you find a machine that had been used for pasta, DO NOT wash it, you will ruin it. The metal rollers are not designed to be washed and will rust, unless you have a stainless steel machine. You will need to roll a waste piece of clay through the rollers until all remaining dough and flour are gone. The pasta machine is used to make even, flat sheets; it has different thickness settings, which is a very useful feature. On its thickest setting, the rollers can be used for kneading two colors together or simply softening the clay, particularly the Fimo brand which is stiffer than the others. The rollers will need to be cleaned between some colors of clay. I do this by placing my towel on top of the rollers and turning the crank to wipe the rollers.

The Food Processor

Another wonderful tool for mixing and softening clay is the food processor. Some food processor brands will work better than others. This is due to the construction of the blade assembly. Look for a processor that has metal parts where the blade joins the motor. The Black and Decker brand "Shortcut II" works well, as does the Westbend model #6491. Plastic parts will not stand up to the stresses of mixing stiff clay. The clay should be broken into small pieces before processing. It may help to add a few drops of mineral oil or plasticizer before processing. Just as you would in the kitchen, turn the motor on and off several times to start the mixing, then, leave it running for a few minutes. The clay will be chopped up into small pieces that turn into little balls. Finally, knead the clay by hand. There really is no substitute for the warmth of your body to soften the clay. As with the pasta machine, don't use the food processor for food afterwards.

12. Tools. Clockwise from the top is an oven thermometer, jeweler's hammer, antique leather wheel, 2 brayers, a grater, 3 types of ceramic tools, 3 types of pin chucks, a collection of leather stamps, blades (2 wallpaper scraper blades and one tissue blade), canape cutters and a pasta machine. In the center, on the left is a collection of dental tools and jeweler's wax working tools, on the right are various scribes and burnishers used by designers, a paintbrush and in the center, an antique ruler.

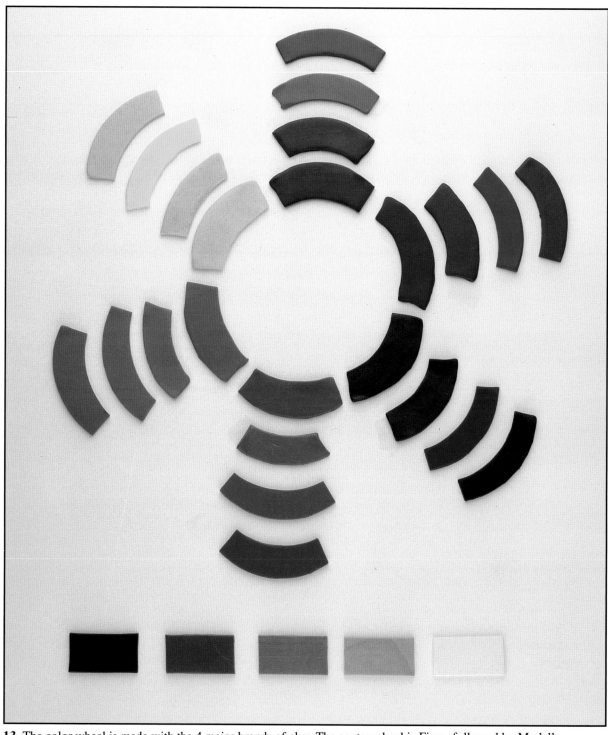

13. The color wheel is made with the 4 major brands of clay. The center wheel is Fimo, followed by Modello, Sculpey III, and Cernit on the outside. The three primaries, red, yellow and blue are unmixed from the package and the three secondaries, green, orange and purple and are made with equal portions of the primaries. Notice that the oranges are really red-oranges. This is because the red pigment is very intense in most brands of clay and you will need to use less of it to achieve yellow orange.

Color

An ideal way to begin working with polymer clay is to do some color mixing. It will help you become familiar with the texture and consistency of the clay as well as begin to learn about how the polymer clay colors behave.

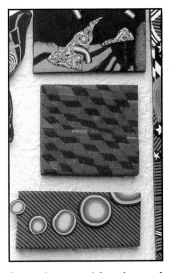

Start to look around your environment at colors. Have you ever had the experience of seeing a distant figure in a pink dress, only to realize, at close range, that she was wearing a white dress with tiny red flowers? Start to notice the way billboards use color. What colors are the letters and the background? They draw your attention and sometimes even appear to vibrate and move. They can be seen easily from a distance, which is often due to the contrast in coloring. This use of contrast is particularly important in small work like jewelry. When you notice small objects, like jewelry on a passersby, the shape is what you notice first, then the overall color, and the pattern is last. If the colors are very similar to one another the pattern becomes lost at a distance.

A pleasing and artistic use of color, and an understanding of contrast, are so important to the success of your work that a review of the basics of color theory is constructive. While everyone has his own preferences for color combinations, there is a science called color theory which attempts to describe and explain how people perceive and react to colors. A mountain of information has been written about the way colors interact with one another, and with the human eye and brain. Color can be studied from the perspective of physics, chemistry, physiology or psychology. The artist is the conscious or unconscious interpreter of knowledge from these disciplines. A brief review of some of these basic concepts, part of the language of art, may inspire you to experiment a bit with color and make some discoveries of your own. The polymer clay colors can be used as they come out of the package, but ultimately you are going to want to make at least some colors of your own. If you keep track of the ratios of clay used to make a specific color, you will be able to reproduce it later. You can pinch off a small amount of the mixed color, flatten it and bake it, then glue it onto a cardboard sheet with the formula noted and you will have a permanent color index.

The Color Wheel

The colors of the rainbow - red, orange, yellow, green, blue and violet - can be arranged in a color wheel. The color wheel is simply a convenient way to represent these spectral colors and relate them to one another. White light is composed of a spectrum of wavelengths that can be seen when the light is separated by a prism or by water in a cloud to produce a rainbow. The light waves themselves are not colored. Color arises in the human eye and brain by translation of the wavelengths into a perception in the brain. It may well be that different people actually perceive colors differently. Objects appear colored to our eyes because as white light [composed of many wavelengths] strikes an object, the object absorbs some of the color wavelengths and reflects back to our eye the unabsorbed ones. The grass is green because green wavelengths are reflected back and all the other ones are absorbed.

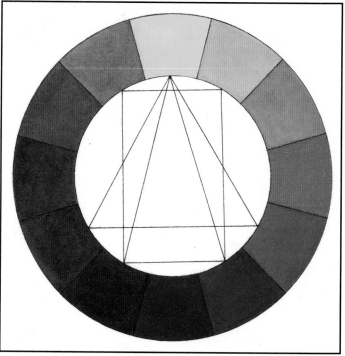

Illustration 2. The Color Wheel. Color harmonies are indicated by the lines within the wheel.

The Primary and Secondary Colors

The primary colors - red, yellow, and blue - are colors that can not be made by combining any other colors. They are non-reducible. Combinations of red, yellow and blue will give all the other colors in the color wheel. Equal parts of red and yellow will give orange. Blue and yellow will give green, and red and blue will give purple. Orange, green and purple are known as the secondary colors. These six colors, the primaries and secondaries, form the basic color wheel. Black and white exist as pigments in paints, but, strictly speaking, are not colors. They are called achromatic or neutral colors.

Hue, Value and Intensity

Hue, value, and intensity are terms that describe various qualities of colors, and also help organize your thinking about color.

The colors in the color wheel and all the other possible colors that can be mixed from them, are called hues. Turquoise, violet, yellow and red-orange are hues.

The term value refers to the lightness or darkness of a specific hue created by adding black or white. The addition of black produces a shade and white added produces a tint. The term value can also be used in another way. The pure, undiluted hues of the color wheel have an intrinsic value or brightness that is not due to dilution with black or white. Yellow is lighter or brighter than blue. In order of intrinsic value on the color wheel, yellow and orange are the brightest, then red and green, lastly blue and purple. The use of different values together will add excitement to your work.

Intensity and saturation are words used to describe the same concept. When a hue is as bright as it can be with no black, white or other color added to dilute it, it is at its maximum intensity - it is fully saturated. The intensity of a particular hue will depend upon the pigment which makes it up. Many of the new, synthetic pigments which are used in paints or polymer clay, are very pure and produce very intense colors. Pigments like alizarine crimson, indigo, or yellow ocher come from plants or minerals, and are very impure. They produce more complex and subdued colors. Some of these plant pigments have been chemically synthesized and, in their purified form, can produce very intense colors. Intensity can also be used in another way. Even when a color is very pure and saturated, it may appear more intense to our eyes. We are able to perceive some colors more easily than others: yellow and red more easily than blue. In addition, much of our color perception is really based on comparison and contrast. Yellow may appear more intense next to black, whereas red will appear more intense next to white.

Complementary Colors and Color Harmonies

Complementary colors are colors that are opposite to one another on the color wheel. Red and green are complements; blue and orange, and yellow and purple are also complementary. Complementary colors used next to one another appear to vibrate and move.

The human eye and brain will perceive a set of colors to be harmonious when they contain a mix of the three primaries on the color wheel - not necessarily in equal parts. Though it might not seem to make sense initially, complementary pairs are considered harmonious by definition because they contain all three primary colors. For example red and green contains red and blue + yellow. In the case of a monochromatic grouping (For example, all shades of blue), the brain/eye wants to compensate for other "missing" colors in the spectrum and the color scheme is less balanced, more weighted and less harmonious.

Another harmonious color combination is described by the idea of split complements, which consists of a hue plus the hues on either side of its complement, ie, yellow plus blue-violet and red-violet. In general, all such triads are harmonious and pleasing no matter where they are on the color wheel. Other harmonies occur on the color wheel by drawing any triangle or rectangle within the wheel. It seems that the brain, when stimulated by one color, "wishes" to be satisfied by a balance of the other colors, producing a "feeling" of harmony. Analogous colors are a set of two or three hues that lie side by side on the color wheel. They may form an analogous harmony of colors, although the palette will be dominated by one hue.

Contrast

The final basic property of color theory to discuss is contrast. This is one of the most useful concepts of all for working with polymer clays. If you are working on a small scale, particularly using the millefiori technique, it is very important to have high contrast in the clay colors in order to see the design. Fine patterns will appear to fuse together when there is little contrast in the colors.

Johannes Itten defines seven basic kinds of color contrast. To fully understand them, you should read his book, but we can briefly go over some of the categories that are easiest to understand. Contrast of hue is the pairing of different pure colors on the color wheel, i.e. red/blue/yellow. Light/dark contrast is also obvious: the blackness or whiteness of colors, like pastels versus somber colors. Cold/warm contrast refers to the pairing of colors which we call warm, like red, orange and yellow, with colors that we call cool, like blue, green and violet. Complementary contrast is the pairing of colors that are opposite on the color wheel. Generally, these also are a warm/cool pair. Simultaneous contrast "results from the fact that for any given color the eye simultaneously requires the complementary color, and generates it spontaneously".[4] This will happen when you stare at a red shape for a period of time and then avert your eyes - green will appear as an after image. This is a brain-generated effect and can not be photographed but can be very powerful visually. This kind of contrast is least likely to apply on a small scale with jewelry. Contrast of saturation is produced by placing intense, pure colors next to dull, mixed colors which are less saturated, like red and yellow next to gray and olive. The final concept is called contrast of extension. It refers to the contrast of volume or area of two color patches - much and little. If a large field of one color, for example green, contains small patches of another color, for example red; the red will appear more luminous and excited than if it were in equal portions with the green. The eye/brain tries very hard to balance the color input and its inability to do so creates a visual excitement. This is the basic

14. A group of four pairs of earrings by Steve Ford and David Forlano of **City Zen Cane**. These pieces are all made from canes. Note the use of gradations of color to achieve dimension. The artists often use colors from the opposite ends of the color wheel to give movement and vibration in their compositions.

principle behind all of these kinds of contrast. You may want to experiment with some of these color ideas.

Throughout his book on color theory, Johannes Itten constantly refers to the subjective and individual reaction of people to color. Color has mystical and psychological significance that may vary between cultures. These things are not quantifiable, and work together with the more scientific and definable concepts to produce the mysterious appeal of art. Art is a language and like any other language it is used to express peoples' inner feelings, but it uses rules and structures that are universal in order to do this. Consciously or unconsciously the mastery of color is fundamental to speaking this language.

Strategies for Color Mixing

Using some of the ideas expressed above, you should develop better skills for mixing colors. Don't let all of this scare you away - it's not necessary to do this scientifically. You will arrive at these same conclusions by experimentation. The idea is to have control over the process and save time. Everyone has his own color palette, and you will want to learn to make colors that you like and use frequently in your own work.

When trying to mix a specific color it is helpful at first to have an example of the color at hand. Hold it up to the color wheel and decide where it would best fit - you are attempting to assign a hue.

An example might be the turquoise color of the gemstone. It is not green or blue but somewhere in between, a blue- green. It does not fall exactly in between the two but has more blue in it. The hue would be blue-blue-green. Start with the brightest blue you have and add a small amount of yellow. Keep adding yellow until you are satisfied that you have a blue-blue-green. Now notice that your clay is darker than the turquoise piece you are trying to match. You will need to add white to it, producing a tint. You may be getting closer to the color now, but it may still seem too bright, not "natural" looking. This is because the intensity is too high. Nature rarely makes colors of high intensity or purity, they are nearly all more subtle, complex mixtures. The way to cut down on the intensity of a color is to mix a tiny amount of its opposite color or complement on the color wheel. In this case it would be orange or red-orange. Take a tiny pinch and mix it into the clay, it should cut the intensity. Now you should be getting closer to the mark and some small adjustments will finish the job. You can try this strategy with any color.

A word of caution: it is much easier to start with the most pure and intense colors of the primaries for mixing though they may seem garish. You will never get a lime green from avocado, because the avocado is already diluted with several other colors. In other words, once you start to mix other colors with a primary color, there is no going back. You will not be able to return to the original primary color.

Some artists, particularly City Zen Cane, have made wonderful use of light to dark shadings of one color to give the illusion of dimension. Generally, this is done by measuring equal amounts of your starting hue, say red, and adding greater and greater amounts of a lighter color like white, to produce a series of shades. These may be layered from dark to light to produce gradual shading. If you add white, however, you may dilute the intensity of the starting color as well as the value. To maintain the intensity, use a pink or pale red to do the diluting instead of white.

Some of the colors are very saturated, like red and black. When working with these colors, use smaller amounts. It will take a large amount of white to dilute red into pink, a tiny pinch of red mixed with white will make a medium pink. Each brand of clay has its own color palette with which you will have to become familiar. It may be almost impossible to mix some colors with some of the brands. Remember that you can intermix the different brands as needed. Experimentation will be the best teacher.

15. The necklace and four pins of FIMO using caneworking by Martha Breen of **Urban Tribe**. The pins are one inch across.

Design

Basic Design Ideas

In every aspect of our vision we impose a brain-driven interpretation of what we perceive as opposed to what is actually there. By taking in images with two eyes we are able to judge depth and distance. Our effort to organize the visual information we take in and interpret can be studied and learned as a set of principles representing the alphabet or tools of art. Understanding these tools, and using them to express the imagery in our minds is, the language of art.

The use of some of these concepts can enhance your jewelry design considerably. At the very least, it may help you to understand why you do or don't like a particular design.

Learning design is learning a new language. Most people have unconsciously absorbed some of this language and can use it without thinking about it, but a real mastery of design principals requires deliberate effort. We are all impacted by design in our daily lives. The world of marketing and sales is concerned with manipulating mood and behavior through visual design. There is an enormous amount written about the subject. These are some of the essential concepts of design that are especially applicable to working with jewelry and polymer clay. Some of the most important design concepts are: proportion, shape, value, depth, color and texture/pattern. All of them are interrelated. When creating an object or painting, you should focus on one or two of these basic concepts. Trying to express too many ideas in any one piece weakens the overall design and dilutes the visual impact. The tools used should be the ones that best express your idea or feeling. For example, strong dramatic emotion might best use bold shapes and pure intense colors. In general, the smaller the art object, the simpler the design should be.

Remember, these concepts are just guidelines and not rules. They can be broken and you can still have an effective design. If you understand and apply these basic ideas, however, you will be more likely to succeed. In general, keep it clear and simple.

Proportion / Division of Space

Proportion is the division of space in a design. An unequal division of space is most interesting. Try to use no more than three major divisions - large, medium, and small - in a given design. Even if using more elements, they should clearly fall within and be a part of the three categories.

Horizontal and vertical divisions of space are static and serene. Diagonals are more dynamic and suggest movement. In a design dominated by diagonals, it is usually more interesting to use some variety in the angles.

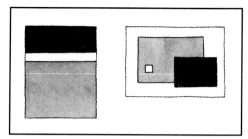

Illustration 3. Division of Space.

Placement

The placement of large, medium and small elements with respect to focal point, symmetry and readability is another important consideration.

Focal Point

You should decide on a definite center of interest. If the focal point is in the center of the design, it can be very static and less interesting. Think of a bullseye pattern. The eye is not encouraged to roam. A dynamic placement is arrived at by dividing the field into thirds horizontally and vertically and noting the intersections, this is where the most effective placement of the focal point will be.

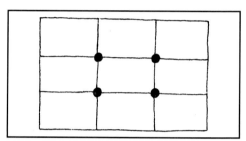

Illustration 4. Placement.

Symmetry/Asymmetry

Symmetrical placement of elements is balanced, static, calm and classical. It may be more difficult to make symmetrical placement exciting, but it can be done by using more contrast in one of the other aspects of the design, like texture or value. Asymmetrical placement is lively and active, suggesting movement and is usually more interesting. This is because the eye/mind is trying to balance the image.

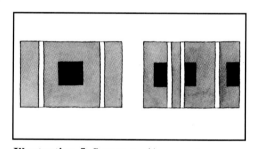

Illustration 5. Symmetry/Asymmetry.

Readability

As Westerners, we decipher a design by entering on the upper left of a field and moving down to exit on the lower right, much as we read text. The focal point or main design elements should lead your eye along this imaginary path. Often we account for this property automatically and are disturbed when a design is turned upside down.

Shape

A variety of shapes, in several sizes, are more lively and interesting than a field containing identical shapes. Try to limit your design to no more than three major shapes in any one design.

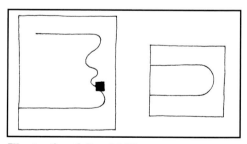

Illustration 6. Readability.

Positive and Negative Space

When thinking of the design format of your object, the design in that space (the positive) and the remaining background (the negative) are equal in importance. Try to make sure your negative space is as interesting as the positive space. This is a good visual exercise to help you see your design elements as not isolated but as relating to the whole field.

Edges

Keeping your design elements unequal distances from the edges will make a more interesting negative shape. Making the shapes that come close to the edge slightly different in angle and placement will create more movement in the field and more interest.

Repetition and Rhythm

Repetition of design elements can create rhythm and movement in the design. The mood of the rhythm is manipulated by the size, shape and placement of the repeated elements - whether all are the same size with random placement, different sizes of the same shape, etc. In general, it is soothing to see elements repeated in an organized pattern and somewhat disturbing to disrupt that order.

Curve/Straight

Curves are soft and organic and generally equate with nature. Straight edges are harder and mechanical and equate with man-made things. Though this concept can be applied to either lines or shapes, we will think in terms of shapes. These elements can help to establish a mood in your design. Depending on the mood that you want to express, a dialogue between the straight line and curve can be very interesting in a design so long as one predominates.

Value

As described in the color section, value refers to the lightness or darkness of a color. Try to work with sets of three basic values: dark, medium and light. Just as with proportion above, a clear contrast between the values adds action and interest to your design. A clear separation of values will allow a design to be read from across a room, even though the detail is not visible. Remember that dark values recede and light values come forward.

Depth

There are three basic ways to achieve depth in a design. Overlapping elements imply depth. This is further enhanced by using overlapping elements of diminishing size or elements of diminishing size alone, and finally, shading. Shading makes use of the properties of value in order to create the illusion of volume, where dark recedes and light

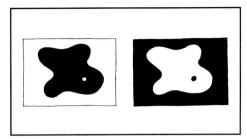

Illustration 7. Positive/Negative Space.

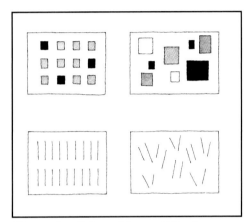

Illustration 8. Repetition and Rhythm.

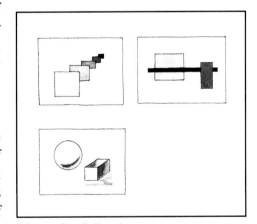

Illustration 9. Depth.

comes forward. All of these properties are the visual cues that we use in nature to assess the volume and distance of objects. We are simply "tricking" the eye into "seeing" three dimensions.

Color

Contrast of color can create a lot of movement and energy in a design. I have discussed these contrasts in the color section above, but I will add an additional point. Any color can be assigned a value. In general, warm colors like red and orange come forward and cool colors, like blue and green recede. These properties can also be used to produce depth with color.

Texture and Pattern

Texture usually refers to a tactile surface, or the illusion of a tactile surface as opposed to a flat pattern which is repetitious. To achieve interest with texture or pattern, use areas of repetition that are changed slightly in the size of pattern or shape, but relate to one another, i.e., changes in the size of the pattern or texture, or changes in the area or shape the texture inhabits. Interesting effects can also be achieved by a contrast between rough and smooth textures.

These are just a few of the most important design guidelines to follow. One, several, or all of these concepts may be at play in any one design. They are used to convey an idea or emotion clearly and effectively to the viewers eye, rather like a language of visual communication. Remember, however, that one design element should predominate. A lifetime could be spent exploring any one of these design elements. Knowing what they are should help you decide how best to express your ideas or remind you of a possible solution when your design seems wrong or uninteresting.

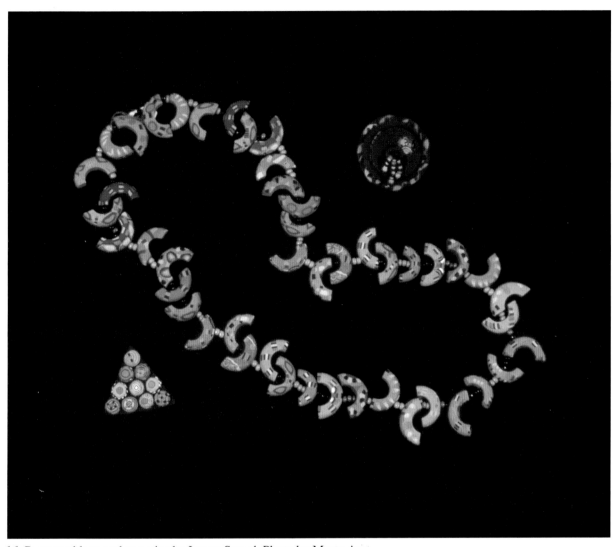

16. Pasta necklace and two pins by Lynne Sward. Photo by Marty Amt.

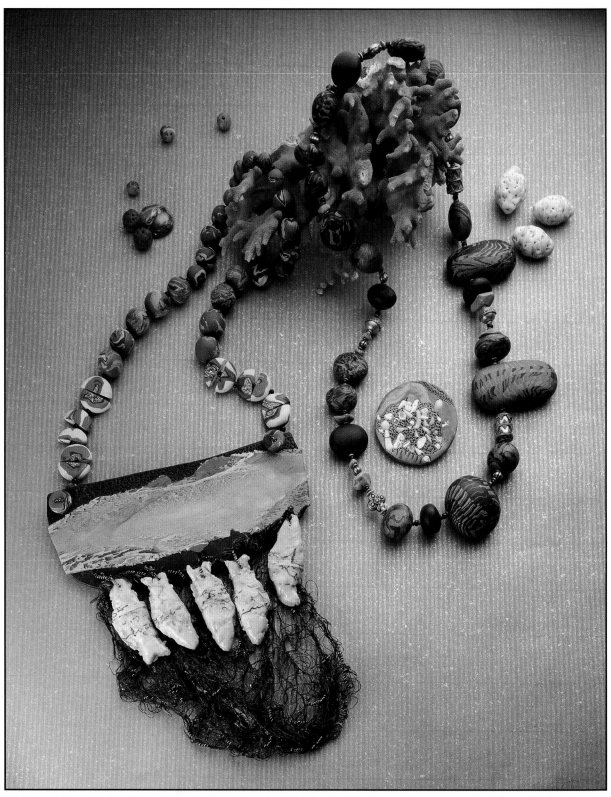

17. The necklace on the left and the circular pin are both by Pat Berlin. The necklace on the right is by Kathleen Dustin. The loose beads are made by Lee Meyers and imitate coral and agate.

Getting Started

Clay Preparation

All the brands of clay must be kneaded before working with them. Some require more work than others and each have their strengths and limitations. I would encourage you to try all the brands and not to be discouraged by the stiffness of some of them. The stiffer clays are generally stronger, and once kneaded, or conditioned, techniques like the reduction of canes (which I will describe later) are not difficult to achieve. Conversely, the softer clays can become mushy and hard to work unless you let the clay "rest" overnight or chill it.

Fimo is the strongest clay and also the most difficult to knead into a working consistency. It is quite stiff when taken from the package and somewhat crumbly, but as you start to knead it, the crumbliness will disappear. This can take two or three minutes of kneading. Once the clay heats up enough from the friction of kneading and the heat of your hands, you can start to roll it with a rolling pin or run it through a pasta machine on the widest setting. The pasta machine is a excellent tool for mixing, as is the food processor for larger quantities.

Sculpey III is very soft out of the package and is easily kneaded to working consistency. This makes it the most accessible product for beginners but it has a drawback: Sculpey can get too soft and mushy if overworked. The remedy is to let it sit overnight or to freeze it. Some people keep a bowl of ice water at the table to cool their hands. A new product, Promat, made by the Sculpey company is more like Fimo in its consistency and is also stronger. Cernit is reported to be as strong or stronger than Fimo, yet it is relatively easy to knead, somewhere between Sculpey and Fimo. Kneading is best done with the hands because your body heat will help warm the clay.

To start kneading, cut or break off a piece of clay and begin to work it into a ball by squeezing. Next, roll it into a cylinder and then pull the two ends of the cylinder, stretching it like taffy, until it breaks. Repeat the process until the clay is soft. As the softest of the clays, Sculpey can be put directly into the pasta machine for mixing or hand kneaded as described above.

The stiffer clays, like Fimo and Pro-mat, may benefit from being pre-warmed. This can be done by putting them in your pocket, sitting on them or placing them on a heating pad. They require a little more patience and hand power but soften up with time. If you try to put Fimo through the pasta machine while cold, it will crumble into pieces. This won't hurt it, just gather up these pieces and knead them into a solid wad. Once you have it softened, flatten the clay a little and then roll it through the pasta machine. Fold the clay in half and run it back through several more times and it will develop a smooth consistency. Be sure to put the fold side in the rollers first to push out air bubbles.

The food processor is one of the fastest ways to get Fimo to working consistency but it is expensive and you must have a good quality processor to stand up to the clay friction. Break the clay into small chunks and turn the processor on. A few drops of mineral oil will aid the process.

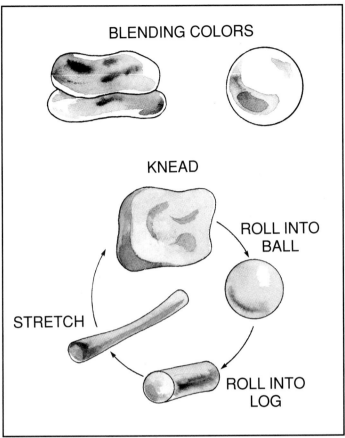

Illustration 10. Clay Mixing.

The clay will eventually turn into small beads. These can then be easily kneaded into a smooth ball, ready for working. Remember that all of the brands of clay may be blended together to optimize color or consistency. (See Photo on opposite page.)

Marble and Imitation of Natural Materials

When two colors are kneaded together they will eventually become one uniform color. Before that happens, however, you will notice a very pleasing marble-like pattern in the clay. You can stop at this point and use the clay in this pattern, which may be reminiscent of marble or other stones. Roll the clay into a snake or cylinder and cut off your first beads. You will notice that there is a random pattern running through the length of the log which is also interesting.

Hand kneading to make marble clay as compared to kneading it with the pasta machine will produce very different effects. Flat sheets that are folded and rolled through the pasta machine will give more uniform striping than hand kneading. (See Photo, page 35)

Stones like agate and malachite can be beau-tifully imitated by polymer clay. Malachite can be made by mixing a dark green color, making several tints, and then kneading or rolling a small amount of white into the green. Once the white has been mixed in, the pasta machine can be used to produce the streaking. Sculpey and Fimo come in a translucent clay that is wonderful to

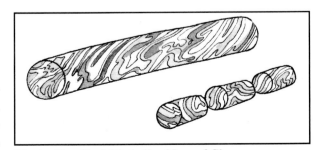

Illustration 11. A Marbelized Log of Clay.

use together with several opaque colors for simulating agate. Many other kinds of natural materials can also be imitated as long as they are opaque - wood, marble, metal, glazed clay, turquoise, coral, bloodstone and many other semiprecious stones.

For wood, try making several different browns, marbleizing them, then pulling the clay to make streaks that imitate wood grain. Texture the surface by taking an impression of real wood grain. The mixing and matching of colors will be very important for a realistic effect.

To make coral, mix the appropriate color and use your needle to pit and score the surface. A sample of the original material will help a great deal when trying to imitate it.

Sandstone can be made by using sandpaper to create a pitted surface texture on appropriate colored clay. See the pin in the upper left in the photo on page 9, by Tory Hughes.

18. Imitation of natural materials. From left to right, marble made by rolling partially blended clay through the pasta machine, lapis lazuli with gold foil blended into the clay, red coral, malachite made by blending three greens and white in the pasta machine, turquoise with silver foil, and agate using transparent clay and earth tones.

19. The round bead. This collection of beads and necklaces is spilling out of a slab-made bowl by **Grove and Grove**. The necklace on the left is by Martha Breen of **Urban Tribe**. The central necklace is by Lynne Sward followed by Kathleen Dustin's *Ladies Bead*. Finally a necklace and bead by Pier Voulkos. The loose beads in the bowl are by Jamey Allen, Lynne Sward, Pier Voulkos, and in the foreground by Nan Roche. One loose bead on the left in the foreground is by Katrina Perry.

The Basic Shapes

Elaboration is the mother of invention, at least in this book. You need master only three basic shapes: the ball, the log or snake, and the sheet. All other processes are based upon elaborations of those shapes. Sounds pretty simple, doesn't it? From these shapes, most other patterns can be made. The formation techniques of each shape will be covered first, followed by a section with a series of more complex elaborations. Many techniques are combinations of several of the basic shapes and these will be explained as we go along.

20. Buttons by Linda Mendelson, using polka dots of laid on color. The largest buttons are 3" in diameter.

The Ball

The first basic shape is the **ball**. To roll a nice even ball shape, take a well- kneaded piece of clay and roll it between your two hands. Roll the clay in your palms while looking between them to check the roundness of the ball. Keep the ball of clay moving in a circular pattern to assure roundness. If you want to make an oval, use an back-and-forth motion between the hands. Use the cup shape of your palm to shape the oval. Don't be discouraged if your balls are not perfectly round to start, this motion is a matter of feel and takes a little bit of practice.

TECHNIQUES WITH BALLS:

Polka Dots

Polka dots are lively design elements for beads and are fun to do. They can be used to imitate "eye" beads, whose magical and mystical meanings reach forward from antiquity. Eye beads are decorated with dots or bull's-eye patterns that are meant to protect the wearer from the "evil eye". In addition, this technique illustrates two of the wonderful properties of this clay: its ability to be layered onto itself, and its ability to fuse into the preexisting color without a trace. This almost magical property allows you play all kinds of visual tricks with your beads.

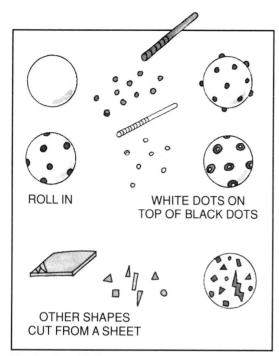

Illustration 12. Polka Dots.

Start by rolling some cherry sized "base" beads of several different colors. To decorate them with polka dots, make some tiny balls, two to three millimeters in diameter, of the colors you used for the base beads and gently stick them onto your bead. [You can also generate dots by slicing a thin piece from a small snake you make by rolling with your fingers.] You can leave the dots raised on the surface or gently roll them into the bead. Try not to be too vigorous with your rolling or your dots will smear. As you roll, the edges of the dots will disappear completely - notice how the dots spread on the surface as they are flattened out. Instead of fusing the polka dots with the bead by rolling you can also press the dots into the bead. This will allow more precision. Now make some dots of the base bead color that are slightly smaller than the previous dots and apply these on top of the preexisting ones. Be sure to center them. Roll them in completely and you will notice an interesting optical effect. The polka dotted surface now looks as if it has a ring on it. The first set of dots has spread even more under the next layer, and because the layers fuse completely, leaving no border, it's difficult to tell how it was made. Remember, if the dots are not round when applied to the bead, the imperfections will grow as the dots spread.

Of course, you can layer any kind of shape onto the surface - triangles, squares, zig-zags, strips or irregular shapes. Take a small piece of clay and flatten it between your fingers; then using your blade cut out shapes. Just remember that they spread according to their thickness; imagine squashing a whole apple versus a cookie shape, the apple will spread much more.

The Log or Snake

The **snake** or **log** is another one of the basic working units for polymer clays. Both fat and thin snakes are used in all kinds of surprising ways. For this reason, it is important to be able to roll a good, even snake and it is not as easy as you might expect. You may have forgotten the impressive skills you had as a child. Now they will come into play again. I will use the word "snake" to refer to smaller diameter, less than pencil thickness, rolls of clay and the word "log" to refer to large rolls.

21. A necklace of polka dot, odd rock beads by Pier Voulkos, 1987.

How to Roll an Even Log

We will start by rolling a fat snake, 3/4 inch thick. Take a ball of kneaded soft clay, place it on your work surface, and begin to roll it with the palm of your hand. Keep your fingers up and out of the way or they will leave a bumpy impression in the log of clay. It is best to use the lower flat part of your hand and roll back and forth with a quick light motion. Let the whole log roll freely. If you press down too hard it will flatten and become bumpy as you roll it. Now roll the fat "log" into a thinner "snake" about pencil thickness. Of course, the log will get longer as you roll it. To keep the snake even, press down the high spots and work up and down the length of the roll, taking your hand off the log and moving it along the entire length. Use a smooth, even motion moving your whole arm while rolling. Try rolling both fat and thin snakes for practice. Of course, as you roll a fat snake into a thin one, the snake will get longer and longer until it becomes unmanageable. Just cut it to a manageable size and keep rolling. Don't be impatient, this takes some practice. Another alternative is to use a small piece of smooth glass or plastic. Place the log on the table and the glass gently on top and roll the log between the two.

Cutting the Log

After you have rolled a nice even snake, you are ready to cut off your first beads. Polymer clay cuts something like semisoft cheese, muenster for instance. It is important to have a clean, sharp blade for good results. [You may want to refer to the chapter on tools for a discussion of blades.] Take your blade in one hand and touch it to the roll where the cut will be made. Do not hold onto the log while slicing, but let it roll freely as you slice with a rolling, sawing motion that rotates the whole log. Press only very lightly or else you will compress the log and get an oval shaped piece.

You must hold the blade perpendicular to your working surface or your slice will not be even. Use your whole arm in the cutting motion. To make beads of the same size, roll a log that is the same thickness throughout and use a ruler to measure off even increments. Each piece, when rolled, will have the same volume of clay and make the same size bead.

Similarly, to make beads of graduated size, measure and cut off segments of graduating size, ie., 1", 1/2", 1/4", 1/8". The beads will be of graded sizes according to the degree of increment. You may also make a log with tapering ends and cut the same length segments and these pieces will also make a graded set of beads.

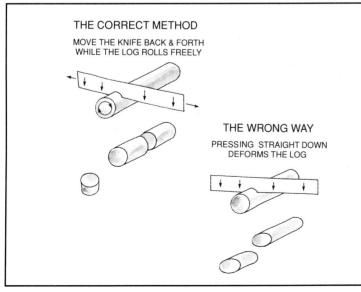

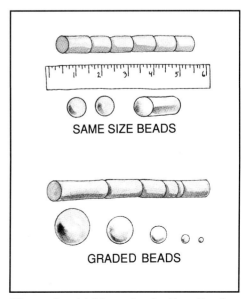

Illustration 13. Cutting a Log Evenly.   **Illustration 14.** Measuring for Even Beads.

Piercing the Beads

Beads are usually pierced before baking, though not everyone does it this way. Some folks drill them with a small drill press or a flexible-shaft jewelers drill, after baking. This may be the preferred method for production work, but some shapes are quite difficult to drill in this way. It is very easy to pierce beads in unorthodox ways when the clay is still soft.

The first beads cut from the log are shaped like cylinders. They can be pierced in several different ways, but the most obvious is to pierce along the barrel of the piece. Piercing the clay is done by holding the bead in one hand between the thumb and first finger. Hold the needle tool in the other hand and rotate the tool, boring through the bead. If you attempt to pierce the clay without rotating the tool, you run the risk of mashing and deforming the bead.

Gentle pressure combined with rotation will do a beautiful job. One trick to give you better control over the trajectory of the needle is to hold the bead between the fingers as shown in the diagram. As you push the needle through there will be an unconscious tendency

22. Three flat rock necklaces and a bracelet by Pier Voulkos, 1989.

to avoid pricking yourself. You will probably have better success if you don't try too hard, this will take some practice. There will be a raised area where the needle exits. Flatten this lip and put the needle back through the other side for a nicely finished hole. As a matter of good craftsmanship, it is worth the effort to nicely finish your beads.

If the above approach doesn't work for you, here is another one. Go into the "north pole" half way with your needle. Pull the needle out and go through the "south pole" all the way, by putting your finger on the north pole and aiming for it. Use a ball point needle so there is no risk of pricking your finger.

The size of the hole should be no larger than the size of the thread or threads onto which the bead will be strung. This is one reason for having a variety of needle sizes on hand. The beads should be held firmly by the stringing material to prevent looseness and floppiness in the finished necklace. Stringing is a subject of its own, and a very important one for a polished, professional look in your jewelry. Refer to the bibliography for a listing of books on the subject. It is

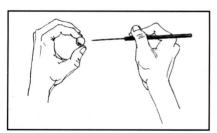

Illustration 15. Piercing a Bead.

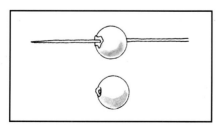

Illustration 16. Pierced Bead.

well worth the effort to take at least one workshop on professional stringing. The chapter on findings will also give you some ideas on how to finish necklaces and other jewelry.

This is a good time to consider the enormous range of possibilities for bead shapes and bead piercing. Beads can come in any size or shape that you can imagine. Unlike glass or stone beads which require skill and expensive equipment to drill, polymer clay beads can be pierced in any way, to suit your purpose. Beads can be pierced once through the center or through just the top part of the bead. With any given shape of bead, there may be many different ways to pierce it to show various faces of the bead. The way beads are pierced and strung can have dramatic textural and structural effects on a necklace. Look at the necklace on page 63 by Pier Voulkos, a necklace by Sara Schriver on page 58, and a necklace by Kathy Amt on page 83, for examples of three very different approaches that can be taken to necklace design.

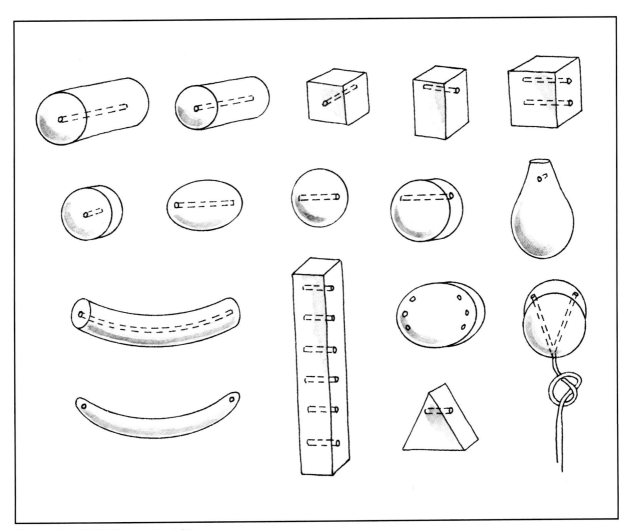

Illustration 17. Different Bead Shapes.

TECHNIQUES WITH SNAKES

Freeform Design

In addition to cutting beads from a log, snakes can be used in a freeform way. For example, long thin snakes can be coiled to make a pendant. Or, logs of different lengths can be cut and pressed together lightly, side by side. Hoops can be made and used in necklaces. The variations are endless.

Surface Decoration

Snakes of varying size can be used as a surface decoration on beads. They can be rolled into the bead completely, where they will spread quite a bit, or they can be left raised on the surface. Light pressure will be enough to cause them to stick. Start with a fat log, as thick as your finger, and cut off several beads. Roll them into balls. Use a slender snake, 1 or 2 mm in diameter, and coil it around the bead. Leave some snakes on the surface of the bead for texture and roll others in.

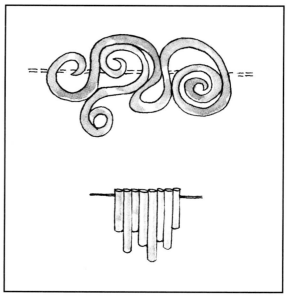

Illustration 18. Freeform Designs.

A small snake can also be laid lengthwise onto a larger log. Just as above, the small snakes can be left on the surface or rolled into the base log. To roll the surface snakes in, roll the log on the table and watch as the laid-on colors begin to spread and flatten on the log. You can stop at any point but, if you continue, the laid-on color will appear to completely fuse with the base log. Notice how much the baby snakes spread out. If they are too fat they will completely cover the base log.

This characteristic to spread can be exploited in some interesting ways. After you have rolled in the first color, lay another finer snake on top of it and roll it in completely. The overlying color will itself spread out and will continue to spread the color beneath it. The effect is one of complex layering and design, yet it is very simple to do.

Wrap Beads

Very simple wrap beads can be made by rolling a snake between your hands and tapering the ends. Use a piece wire and coil the snake around it like a spring and bake them together. The wire can be pulled out after baking.

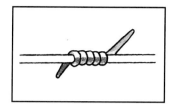

Illustration 19. A Wrapped Bead.

Your First Cane

The word **cane** is borrowed from glassworking traditions, where it refers to a rod, or log, of glass with a pattern running through the length of it, much like a jellyroll. In the Venetian glass industry, these canes are used to decorate beads. This is done by slicing small pieces or "cookies" of glass from the rod and melting them onto a base bead. The Venetian glass trade beads called millefiori are made in this way. Polymer clays are ideal for imitating this process. See photo on page viii for an example.

With this in mind, you can construct a simple, random cane very easily. Roll some pencil thick logs in seven different colors. Choose a color for the center and arrange the others around it. Roll them together until they fuse into a solid cane. Now for the magic! Take your blade and slice off one of the ends. A pattern of color appears. Notice how the round logs of color have spread into the spaces forming a mosaic where all the borders are fused with one another. Watch for this effect in other techniques.

Slices or cookies can be cut from the cane to make tabular beads. Larger pieces can be cut as cylinders, pierced, and used as beads themselves or, these pieces can be rolled into balls where the pattern will show on two sides. Very thin pieces can be used to decorate the surface of beads or other pieces.

If you cut slices from your striped cane, try taking a slice and flattening it with your thumb on a small piece of wax paper. Notice that the side stripes make a starburst pattern when the clay is flattened. The thicker the slice, the greater the extent of the starburst. If your cane is rolled in metallic powder before slicing and you flatten the slice as above, a metallic ring will appear. You can make tabular beads using a slice of your cane placed on a base piece of clay and make very effective use of this consequence. Look at photo 52 on page 78 for an example.

Another option is to reduce the diameter of the cane by rolling. I call this reduction. If you roll the cane down to a smaller diameter and slice the baby cane, you will find the pattern intact as it had been, but miniaturized.

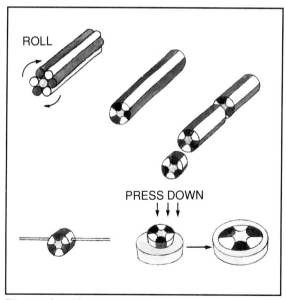

Illustration 20. A Simple Cane.

If some of the colors are smeared where you have cut, it's because the clay was too soft from the heat of your hands. This is especially true when using Sculpey. You can put your cane in the freezer for 15 minutes to cool it before slicing, but the best strategy is to rest the clay overnight to allow it come to a uniform, cooler temperature. If you still have problems, your slicing technique may also be at fault. You may be pressing too hard or not have your blade perpendicular to the cane, or the blade may not be sharp enough.

Filler Beads

These little beads are quick and easy to make and are very attractive fillers between larger beads. They remind me of Heishi beads of the Native American Indians which are made of thin slices of shell that are pierced and strung and then ground to a round shape. To make them from clay, roll a very even pencil-sized log. Cut it into 3/4 inch lengths. Pierce each length along the barrel and thread it onto a very straight wire. The log needs to be consistent in thickness and the hole should be bored evenly through the center of the log. Next, slice the log in even increments while it is still on the wire. Allow the whole log, wire and all, to rotate on the table as your blade slices through. The wire will stop the blade. It must be very straight and you must

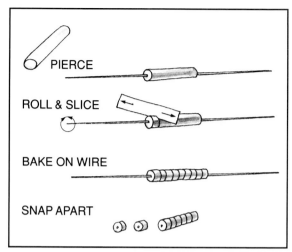

Illustration 21. Filler Beads.

hold the blade perfectly perpendicular to get an even cut. Leave the sliced log on the wire and bake it "as is". When the beads are cooled, they will snap apart into thin disks. Slip the whole log off the wire. You may need to use a small jeweler's plyers to snap apart very thin disks. This is a technique which will take a little practice to master, but it is worth it because you can make beautiful little filler disks in large numbers.

Folded Beads

This wonderful technique was rediscovered and applied to the polymer clays by Jamey Allen. As a bead researcher, he comes across many rare beads and tries to determine how they were made. Many ancient Middle Eastern beads from which this technique was derived, would have remained a real mystery were it not for the use of polymer clay and its unique ability to mimic glass. It will be very helpful to refer to the photograph as you try this. Start out by rolling a snake, about five inches long, with stripes running the length. Join the log into a ring. Shape the ring into a triangle and now, along each length of the triangle, rotate the clay so that the striping twists. You must hold and stabilize two corners with one hand, while you rotate a side with the other. Pinch each corner

23. Three Persian folded beads, 500 - 1000 AD, Early Islamic Period, Syria formerly from the collection of Dr. William K. Ehrenfeld. Photographed by Jamey D. Allen.

of the triangle together, forming a "Y" shape. Pull the arms of the "Y" up together, like a flower folding up. Gently roll the bead together. Obviously, the more varied and complex your striping is on the original snake, the more elaborate the bead pattern will be.

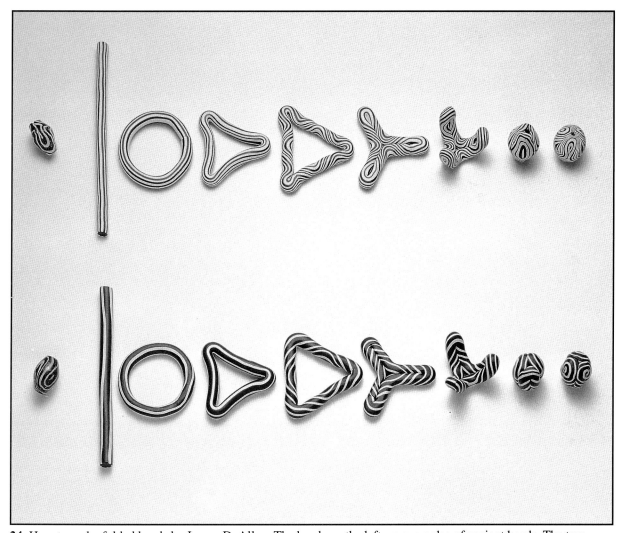

24. How to make folded beads by Jamey D. Allen. The beads on the left are examples of ancient beads. The two completed beads to the right of the series show the variation resulting from folding the floret up as shown or in the opposite direction.

25. A necklace made by Jamey D. Allen using a variety of folded beads as well as surface cane decorations.

Checkerboard

A checkerboard can be made out of snakes. Roll two snakes of contrasting colors about 1/4" in diameter. Cut five even pieces about two inches long from each snake. Arrange the snake pieces as shown in the drawing, by alternating the dark and light pieces. Press the loaf together, maintaining the square form, and use your brayer to flatten the sides. This will produce a loaf that has a crude check pattern. More precise checks will result if the snakes are squared off before assembling. A much easier and more precise way to make a checker board will be discussed in a later section.

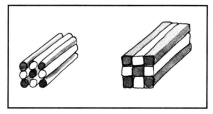

Illustration 22. A Checkerboard Made with Logs.

26. The candy cane or twist is the theme of this grouping. The totemic figure, *Man*, is by Debra Banyas and the necklace is by Kathleen Dustin. The loose beads in the foreground are by Jamey D. Allen. The shell beads are made by Nan Roche and are inspired by the beads of Katrina Perry.

Candy Canes (Twisted Logs)

Another basic variation using the log is the **candy cane**. Because of the properties of the clay, amazing things can be done with this technique. It requires a little practice to get really even canes, so be patient with yourself.

Start out with two pencil-thick snakes of different colors. Highly contrasting colors will show up best. Lay the snakes side by side. Hold one end of the pair with a finger. Now, gently pull downwards and twist both of the snakes together. You want the two snakes to

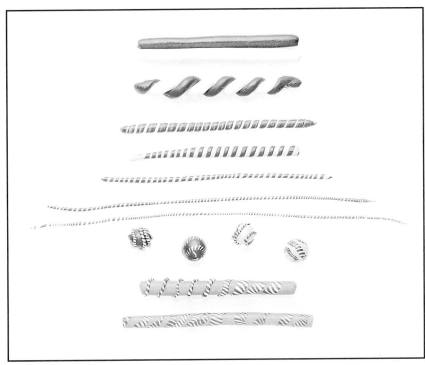

27. A series of twisted candy canes showing the canes applied to different surfaces and rolled in.

wrap equally around each other as opposed to one wrapping around the other. Keep holding one end and continue twisting. Stop twisting and roll the cane together as described above, until the two colors fuse. You will notice that the twists get finer and finer. Keep the twisted log as even as possible. Alternate between twisting and rolling the clay together until you generate a finer and finer candy cane. The more you twist, the closer together the stripes will become and the more you roll, the more the stripes will spread. With a little practice, you can make very fine candy canes. An alternative method is to join the two colors into one cane by rolling and then to twist it into a candy cane. These two methods will give slightly different results.

If the cane gets too long for you to roll easily, or you get a thin area, cut it to a manageable size and continue twisting. If one of the colors is softer, it may stretch a little more and have a tendency to encase the other color. When this happens, the softer color will cover over the other color and your candy cane will not have even stripes. To avoid this, make sure the clay is about the same stiffness before starting. Wonderful things happen even though the candy canes are not perfectly even.

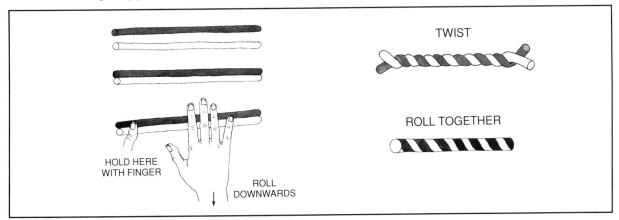

Illustration 23. The Candy Cane.

As a variation, candy canes can be made with more than two colors. They can also be made with snakes of non-equal thicknesses. One of the elements of the candy cane can itself be a candy cane. Try slicing open one of your larger candy canes lengthwise, like a hotdog bun. A wonderful surprise awaits you. Play around and see what happens.

TECHNIQUES WITH CANDY CANES

Surface Decoration

Try using your candy canes to decorate some beads. Make a base bead out of each of the colors that are in your candy cane. Take a small section of candy cane and wrap it in a free form design on the surface of each bead as you see in the illustration. You can stop at this point and leave the decoration raised above the surface. But, a very interesting thing happens when you roll the cane into the bead. Roll very gently at first until the cane begins to fuse with the bead. Continue rolling until you can no longer see any borders. Notice that the candy cane spreads quite a bit. The final effect will be one of a ladder-like array of stripes on the surface of the bead.

The same sort of decoration can be applied to a log, either by laying the candy cane along the length of it, by twisting it around, barber pole fashion or by fusing the candy cane with the log and then twisting.

Another approach is to use the candy canes as surface design without rolling the cane in. Cutting off a small barrel as a base bead, apply strips of candy cane lengthwise on the barrel. If you make several candy canes with opposite twists and alternate them on the bead you will get a mock chevron pattern. The variations are unlimited: for example, the cane can be wrapped around the body of the bead, or a tiny piece can be used around the pierced hole of the bead. It's very elegant to finish off a bead in this way. Candy canes can be used as a perimeter decoration around the edges of a broach or earrings or the lip of a vase. They can be used in any place where you might want to hide a joint.

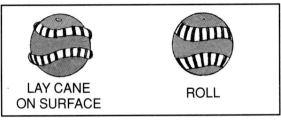
LAY CANE ON SURFACE   ROLL

Illustration 24. Candy Cane Bead.

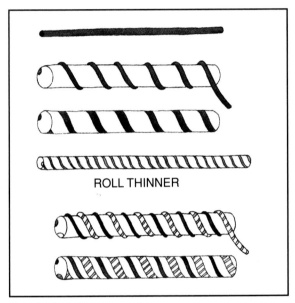
ROLL THINNER

Illustration 25. Wrapped Logs.

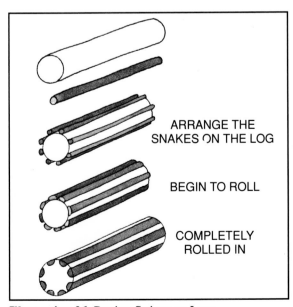
ARRANGE THE SNAKES ON THE LOG

BEGIN TO ROLL

COMPLETELY ROLLED IN

Illustration 26. Putting Stripes on Logs.

Disk Beads

Another interesting type of bead to make with candy canes is a little disk bead with a border of twist. Roll a pencil-thick log and cut off an 1/8 inch slice. Use a thin piece of your candy cane and wrap it around the perimeter of the bead. Pierce the bead through the flat side of the disk. A whole row of beads decorated this way makes a very lively and interesting strand of beads.

Shells

Various kinds of coiled shells can be imitated very easily using tapered snakes. I first saw beads like this made by Katrina Perry. To get a very fine stripe in the cane, put a baby snake along the length on one side only. Then, twist the whole log. Taper one end into a very fine snake by rolling. Start at that end and begin to coil the snake into a nautilus shape. The more pronounced the taper from one end to the other, the better the shape will be.

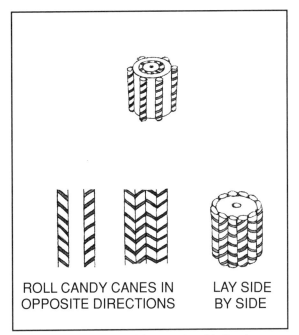

ROLL CANDY CANES IN OPPOSITE DIRECTIONS   LAY SIDE BY SIDE

Illustration 27. Other Things to do with Candy Canes.

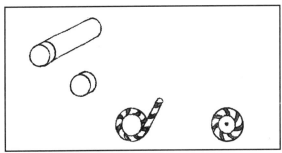

Illustration 28. Disk Beads.

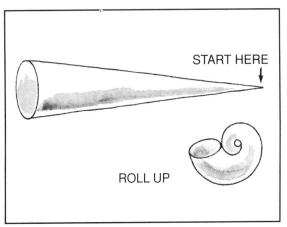

START HERE

ROLL UP

Illustration 29. Shell Beads.

28. A series of pieces using sheets of clay either as a base layer to be built upon or using sheets to build up geometric canes which are then sliced and layered onto a backing piece. Starting at the upper left corner are three pins: the black and white pin and the heart are by **City Zen Cane** and the red squares are by **Grove and Grove**. The jumping jack *Weight Lifter* is by Kathy Amt and is built onto a backing slab of Promat. The necklace is by **City Zen Cane.** The two pins in the lower left and the center are by **Grove and Grove** and show the possibilities for bending and pleating the clay like fabric. The earrings in the lower left are by Lynne Sward.

The Sheet

The third basic shape is the **sheet**. It can be used alone or in combination with other shapes to make jewelry, vessels, or clothing on dolls. Sheets can be freely formed to make pins or necklace elements, or layered together to make striped blocks. A sheet can be wrapped around a grouping of snakes and rolled into one unit, forming a cane, or become the nose on a fair maiden's face.

First, we'll look at the various ways to form sheets, then we will follow some examples of ways to work with sheets. As before, you will see how simple techniques can be elaborated upon and combined to yield patterns that look very complex but are really very easy to make.

Sheet Formation

There are several ways to make a sheet of polymer clay. You can use your hands, a smooth, round drinking glass, a rolling pin, a printing brayer or a pasta machine.

If a perfectly even sheet of clay is not required, the hands are a very quick and effective tool. Start with a soft, well-kneaded piece of clay. Press it between your two hands and flatten and press the clay as though you were making pizza dough. Use the palms of your hands, not your fingers because they will leave ridges on the clay. When the clay is cookie shaped you can slap it back and forth between your two hands rotating it slightly each time. The clay is somewhat stretchy, like pizza dough, and will become larger around and thinner using this motion.

If a more even sheet of clay is needed, use a rolling pin, or a smooth, round drinking glass. If the rolling pin is wooden, it will leave a texture on the sheet of clay and the clay may stick to the wood. The best rolling pin to use is a marble or stone pastry pin, as the clay is less likely to stick and acquire a texture. Again, start with a well-kneaded wad of clay. Flatten it out a bit with your hands and place it on a surface to which it won't stick, like Formica, or a plastic sheet. Using your rolling pin or glass start to roll out the clay just as you would cookie dough. Roll first in one direction, then in the other. When you have rolled it out evenly you should be able to pull it up at one edge and peel it up

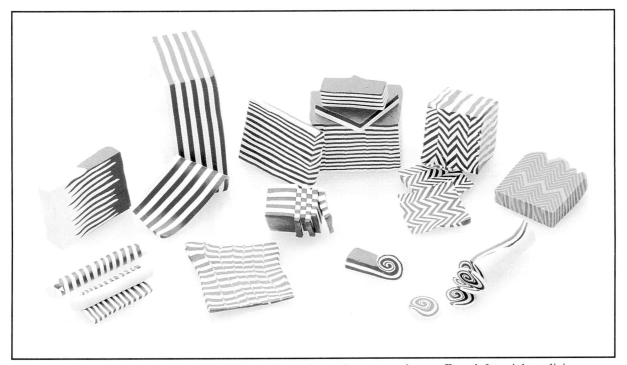

29. Examples of different ways in which slabs can be used to make canes or loaves. From left to right, splicing, striped loaves, feathering, a checkerboard loaf, a chevron loaf, and a jellyroll.

off the surface. It may stretch a little, but this won't hurt anything. Sometimes a piece of wax paper taped onto a surface is the best solution because the whole thing can be picked up and the wax paper can be peeled from the back of the sheet of clay. Turn the piece over often to prevent sticking.

A printing brayer or wallpaper roller can also be used to roll out clay. Though brayers are not as wide as a rolling pin they are a big help for small-scale work or for making small pieces to apply onto larger works.

A pasta machine is the quickest and easiest way to get an even,

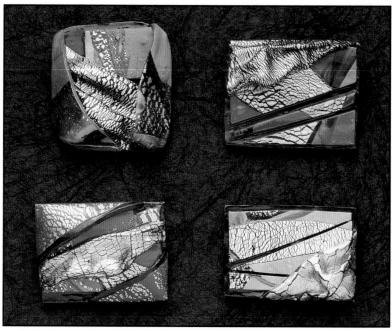

30. Four pins by Kaz Yamashita using gold and silver foils. The artist's use of the clay as a fabric is consistent with a background in fiberarts.

consistent sheet of clay. Form the clay into a rectangular shape and place it in the machine lengthwise. Remember, Fimo must be warm and well conditioned, first. This will give you the widest sheet when you roll it through. Most machines have different settings for thickness. Start out with the thickest setting. You may want to roll it through several times to soften and mix the clay. Fold it in half, before rolling it through. As you do this, always place the fold side into the machine first. This will squeeze out the air between the layers as the clay moves through the machine. You can continue rolling the clay through successively thinner settings until you get a paper-thin sheet that is as flexible as a piece of fabric. Once you have some sheets of different thicknesses in several colors, there is an enormous range of things you can do with them.

TECHNIQUES WITH SHEETS

Freeform Folding

Clay that has been rolled very thin has the feel of fine leather. Thin sheets of clay can be gathered, pleated and folded just like cloth. The pins of Kaz Yamashita (above), Grove and Grove on page 52, and the clothing on Maureen Carlson's Wee Folks on page 102, are all examples of this technique. Start with kneaded, warm clay. Roll it through the pasta machine, changing the settings, until it is as thin as you want it. Drape and form the clay while it's still warm, to avoid cracking. For example, you can make a fan shape by pleating a rectangle of clay along one edge. Pinch it lightly at the base, bake it, and attach a pin back with glue after it has cooled.

A piece of cloth can be pressed onto the clay adding surface texture to imitate cloth even more. You might try coarse burlap, linen, fine muslin, or even brocades for texture. Remember, the thinner the clay, the more likely that it will burn if your temperature is too high, so watch it carefully. Refer to the section on baking on page 12.

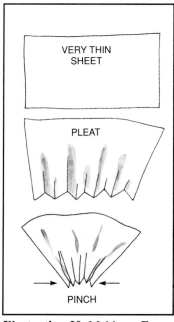

VERY THIN
SHEET

PLEAT

PINCH

Illustration 30. Making a Fan.

31. The necklace is from the *Spanish Skirt* Series by Jeanne Sturdevant. Notice the use of wrapped sheets of clay to form the beads. The earrings are called *Aerial Landscape* and the cameo pin is titled *Serena*.

32. The necklace, earrings and pin are by Lindly Haunani Miller. Thin strips of colored clay are laid onto the black background bead and rolled in. The earrings and pin are made from canes.

Flatwork

Sheets of clay can be used to make jewelry by simply cutting out shapes and applying them onto a base piece of clay. Tory Hughes stamp pins are made this way. (See the photo on page 9 and the photo on page 98.)

Try making a pair of earrings. Start out with two identical shapes from a relatively thick sheet of clay. You can use a template of paper or cardboard around which to cut. Roll out some sheets of several other colors and cut some smaller geometric shapes. Arrange them on the square in a pleasing way. Apply light pressure to the pieces to help them stick. Textures, stamps, foil, glitters, and found objects can be added.

To cut round or irregular shapes, you can use an old medicine bottle or canape cutters. The canape cutters look like miniature cookie cutters and can be found at your gourmet kitchen store. Look at the tool photo on page 19 for examples.

33. An example of simple sheetworking using cut out pieces laid onto a backing piece of clay.

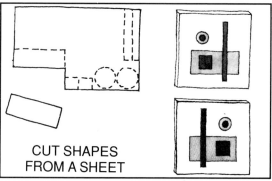

CUT SHAPES
FROM A SHEET

Illustration 31. Flatwork.

34. *Iridian Faces* by Ellen Watt of **Wear Art** using applied and textured pieces of clay and collage elements.

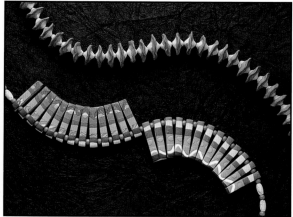

35. Two necklaces by Cathy Glasson of **Art Necko**. The bib necklace has laid on color pieces and is reversible. The rippled disk necklace was inspired by the shape of guinea pig ears.

Marquetry

Another way to approach flatworking comes from the woodworking technique called **marquetry**. Marquetry is a method that uses inlaid pieces of wood veneer to create an image or pattern. The wood pieces are cut and shaped to fit each other like a puzzle or patchwork quilt. This same technique can be used with clay. Completed marquetry images can be set into a wooden box or furniture, or used as is for jewelry. For inspiration, look at the tremendous diversity of patchwork patterns available in books. Cut regular shapes, like triangles, from a sheet of clay and piece them together on a backing sheet. If you use a sheet of clay that has a directional grain pattern blended in, the pieced marquetry can incorporate this pattern in the design. In woodworking, the marquetry piece would be sanded smooth on the surface when completed. To achieve this same effect with polymer clay, use your brayer to gently smooth the surface.

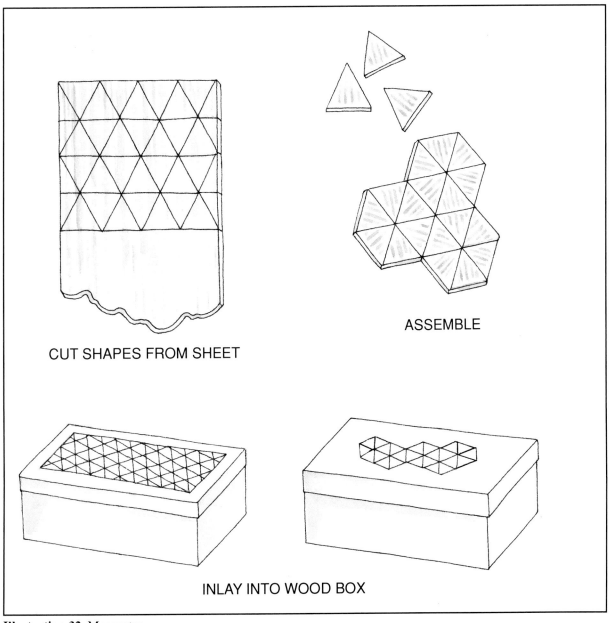

CUT SHAPES FROM SHEET

ASSEMBLE

INLAY INTO WOOD BOX

Illustration 32. Marquetry.

36. A necklace by Sara Shriver. Notice the artist's use of imagery in a variety of shapes and combinations.

Jellyrolls

Remember making a jelly roll with your grandmother? This is another application for sheets of clay. Take two (or three) sheets of different colors. Cut one large rectangle of the same size out of each piece. The rectangle should be at least 2 1/2 times longer than it is wide. Flatten one short end using your brayer or rolling pin, making a long, thin taper. Place one piece on top of the other, staggering them slightly. Start at the tapered end and tightly roll them up. Continue to roll the log with your hand, just as you did before, pressing it together. You can cut off a one inch piece of the log and continue to roll it out, thinner and thinner, making a smaller version of the original pattern. Clean up your ends by slicing them off and the jelly roll will appear in perfect miniature! Remember to use a sawing, rolling motion with light pressure as you cut. Don't mash down. Actually, you need not taper the ends to roll them or stagger them, but the jellyroll effect will be somewhat different with each method. Try different approaches.

These pieces can be used in many ways. Cut off several long cylinder-shaped pieces from the log and pierce them for beads. The pattern shows on the end. The barrel pieces can also be rolled into round beads. Thin slices of the log can be pressed onto a backing piece to make tabular beads. Try stringing several shapes of beads with the same pattern together. This is far more interesting than a string of identical beads. Notice the use of jelly roll canes in the necklaces by Sara Shriver on the previous page.

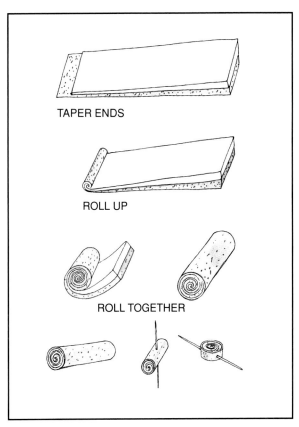

Illustration 33. The Jelly Roll.

Stripes and Plaids

In keeping with the food analogy, the next approach is similar to a layer cake. We'll start out with a loaf of even stripes and then elaborate. Striped loaves can be used in an enormous number of ways: on their own, grouped together, or as components of more complicated images. A lot of variation is possible. The stripes can be thick or thin, in many layers or a few bold lines, and in any combination of colors.

Simple Stripes

For simple stripes, roll out several sheets of two different colors. Use the thickest setting on the pasta machine for both. Cut 2" x 2" squares, five of each color. Next, layer every other color. You now have what we'll call a **loaf**. Pick it up and gently press it together from the center outward. You can also use a brayer to smooth the top. Now trim off the sides to tidy up the loaf. To do this, take your blade in both hands. Slice down through the loaf as though it were a block of cheese, holding the blade perpendicular to the loaf and resting your wrists on the table for stability. If the pattern smears, the clay is still too warm and soft. The loaf should be allowed to "rest" overnight. You can also try freezing it for an hour or so to stiffen it. Stand the loaf up and cut straight down to trim the edges holding the knife perpendicular to the edges of the loaf.

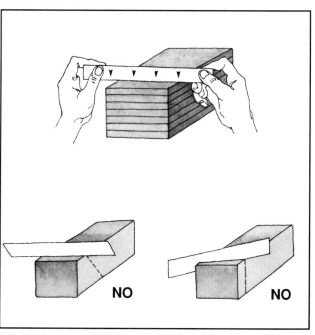

Illustration 34. Slicing a Loaf Evenly.

Just as you did with the logs, you can reduce the loaf by pressing, pinching, or rolling to produce a smaller loaf. Try compressing your loaf from the top only, to half the original height, then cut it in two and stack these pieces to give you a loaf of the same height with twice the number of stripes. Repeat this again until you get four times the number of stripes in the same thickness.

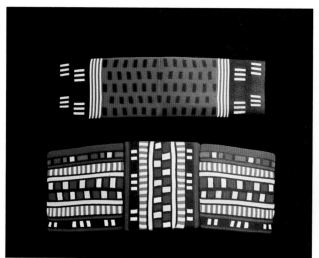

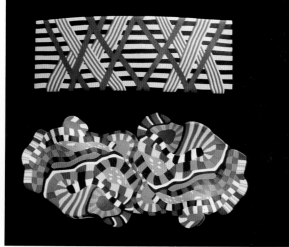

37. Four barrettes by **Grove and Grove** ranging in design from controlled geometric designs to freeform patterning.

The resulting block may also be called a **stratified mosaic** block, a term used by Jamey Allen. A stratified loaf can also be made in another way, producing a slightly different effect. Take two balls of clay the same size and equally soft. Place one on top of the other and squash them into a flat pancake. Press the edges into a square, and keep squashing the pancake flat. You can add more layers and trim the loaf as before.

Remember the layer cake? Your stripes don't have to be the same thickness. Sheets of different thicknesses can be put together into a loaf. For wider stripes than the pasta machine setting, put two sheets of the same color together. The join will not show if they are pressed together well. With all of these layering techniques, take care to prevent air bubbles from becoming trapped between the layers. When you bake the pieces, trapped air will expand and a bubble will form.

Striping is often more interesting when geometric ratios are used for the thickness of the stripes. This is an old weavers' trick for making stripes and plaids more interesting. Examine a piece of plaid cloth and notice the width and sequence of the stripes. There are innumerable patterns that can be made using striped loaves. Look at the work of City Zen Cane and Grove and Grove on pages 24 and 60. Let's elaborate.

Once you have made a striped loaf, you can cut it up and rearrange it in any way. Follow along by looking at the drawings. After trimming all four sides, cut the loaf into four equal pieces. Leave two of the pieces in the horizontal position and tip two of them into the vertical position. Reassemble the horizontal and vertical pieces into one loaf as shown in the drawing. Press the loaf together with your fingers or a brayer. This loaf can now be stretched into a longer, thinner piece, again cut into four pieces and reassembled into a more intricate loaf. Does it remind you of a patchwork quilt? Patchwork patterns are an excellent source of inspiration.

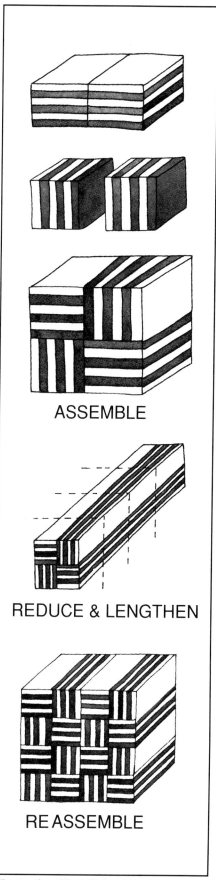

ASSEMBLE

REDUCE & LENGTHEN

RE ASSEMBLE

Illustration 35. A Striped Loaf.

Pinwheel

Let's try another variation. This one is called a pinwheel. Start with a loaf of stripes as before, and a block of clay of a third color, approximately the same size. The blocks should be about 1" by 2" by 1" high. For the solid color, use your brayer to flatten the sides and top of the loaf. Trim all faces of both loaves. Take the striped loaf and tip it so that the striped face is "staring up" at you. Cut the block in half. You should have two roughly one inch cubes. Now, cut each of the cubes on a diagonal. Cut the solid block in the same manner. All the pieces should be the same size. Assemble the solid colored pieces with the patterned pieces to produce four squares that are half color and half pattern. Put these four pieces together to form a pinwheel. You'll now have a loaf that is 1" thick by 2" square on the face.

Again, try reducing the loaf to half the diameter. Start compressing the loaf with your fingers, first on one side and then the other, stretching slightly as you pinch. Don't press too hard. Use gentle, even pressure on all faces. You should expect this to take some time - don't rush it. The brayer is also useful for this task. The more careful and patient you are, the better will be the results. The ability to reduce a pattern in this manner is one of the most wonderful properties of this material, and will be discussed in more detail in the chapter on the cane. As you reduce the diameter, all of the detail is retained in perfect miniature. Any loaf of any shape or size can be transformed by working it into another size or shape, often with surprising results.

Plaid

Plaid is also a possibility. Follow the drawing, this time starting with a loaf with stripes of varying sizes. Slice the loaf vertically in two places and insert two sheets of clay as shown. Reassemble the loaf. As before - you can reduce the loaf, making it longer, and cut it into four pieces along its length to reassemble it into a more complex pattern, as shown in the drawing.

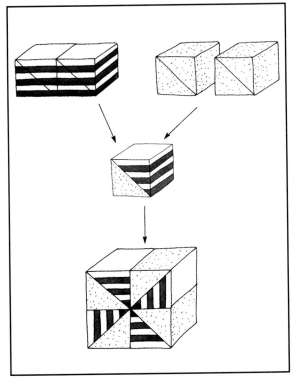

Illustration 36. A Pinwheel Loaf.

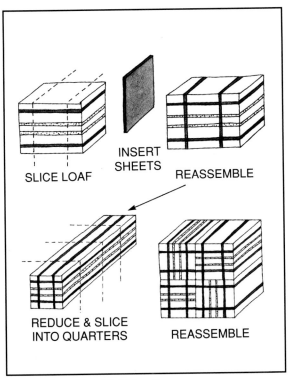

Illustration 37. A Plaid Loaf.

38. A necklace by Pier Voulkos using canes that are made by splicing sheets of color together.

Splicing

This is a variation on the striped loaf described above except that the stripes don't go all the way through the loaf. For this pattern roll some sheets of two colors and cut rectangles of the same size. Flatten one edge of each sheet. The flattened edges will point into the loaf as you assemble it, with the colors alternating. The middle of the loaf will be thicker initially but just keep pressing the layers together until the loaf is the same thickness throughout. Trim the ends to see the pattern. The loaf can be shaped into a different shape or rolled into a log and the pattern will remain essentially the same. This technique has been used beautifully by Pier Voulkos in a necklace on page 63.

Chevrons

This pattern is made with a loaf of even stripes. Tip the loaf so that the stripes are "looking up" at you from your working surface. Slice through the entire loaf on the diagonal, making cuts of the same thickness. Make sure you slice evenly down through the loaf. If your clay is too warm, let it "rest" for a while or this will be a frustrating technique to attempt. Assemble the pieces by turning every other piece upside down and flipping it over, laying it next to the first piece. You may not get this to work immediately but keep playing with your pieces until they match up to form chevrons. Shift the pieces slightly to line up the dark and light stripes, matching them up as well as possible on both sides. Compress the new loaf and trim off the excess irregular ends. Don't worry if this doesn't work the first time, the pattern will be wonderful anyway. It takes a lot of practice to have perfect mastery over these geometric patterns.

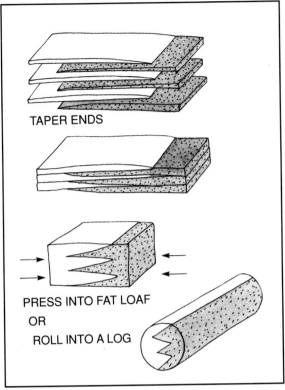

Illustration 38. Splicing.

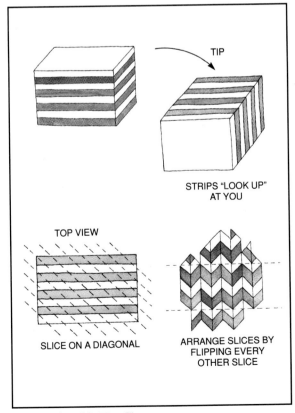

Illustration 39. The Chevron.

39. Two vessels by **City Zen Cane**. Slices of canes have been laid onto PVC piping and baked, the surface is then sanded and polished.

Color Shading

Another variation on the layer-cake idea, is used extensively by City Zen Cane in their work. Using many fine sheets of progressively lighter colors produce an illusion of dimension.

To try this out, you will first need to mix a series of tints of one color. You can use any color, but I will illustrate this with shades of red. Start with five walnut- sized balls of kneaded white clay. You will be mixing progressively larger amounts of red (or any other color) to make many shades of pink. Next, roll a log of red clay about pencil thickness. Using a ruler, measure these five lengths on the log: 1/8", 3/4", 2 1/4", 3" and 4 1/2". [When you use another color, the proportions will be different based on the saturation; experiment with them.] Mix each piece of red with the balls of white clay, producing five shades of pink. Use undiluted white and red as the sixth and seventh color. Roll each color into a sheet and layer the sheets in sequence from

40. *Watermelon* necklace and *Kimono* pin are by Lindly Haunani Miller.

white through pink to red. Trim the resulting block on all faces. The illusion of shading will become more intense as the loaf is reduced in size. The loaf can be cut and arranged so that it goes from dark to light to dark again. This will give an illusion of dimension. Remember the design rules? Dark colors recede and light colors come forward. An infinite number of patterns can be used by cutting and rearranging the loaf as shown in the drawing or combining it with other patterns.

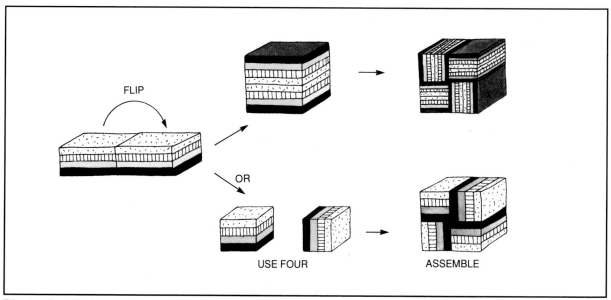

FLIP

OR

USE FOUR

ASSEMBLE

Illustration 40. Several Ways to Arrange a Shaded Loaf.

Feathering

This technique is borrowed from the glassworking world. **Feathering** is the process of dragging a pointed tool through molten stripes of colored glass. To make this pattern in polymer clay, start with a slice from your black and white striped loaf. Using a needle, score across the stripes with light pressure. Use a roller to flatten the clay. As shown in the drawing, you may stroke first in one direction and then in the opposite direction to produce a feathered pattern.

41. A collection of feathered and trailed Venetian glass beads made by applying colors and pulling a pin through the molten glass.

42. A combed glass bead courtesy of the Smithsonian Institution, Freer Gallery of Art, Washington, DC. Accession number 09.921 diameter 1". Photographed by Marty Amt.

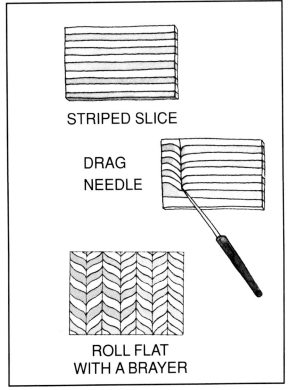

STRIPED SLICE

DRAG NEEDLE

ROLL FLAT WITH A BRAYER

Illustration 41. Feathering.

Checkerboards

The checkerboard is yet another seemingly complex pattern that is easy to make with a block of stripes. There are two approaches using a black and white loaf as described above, and a looser method using snakes (described on page 47). After making your striped loaf, tip the block so that the stripes are "looking up" at you from your working surface. Using your blade, cut slices from the block that are the same thickness as the stripes in the loaf. For the first method, stagger the slices so that the black and white squares line

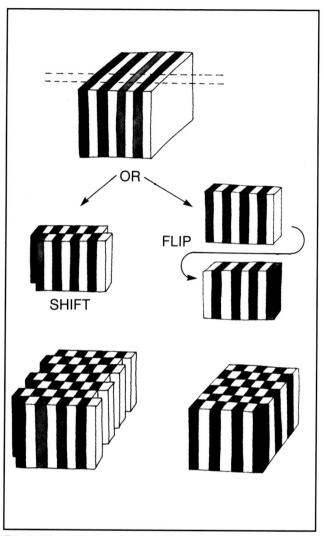

Illustration 42. The Checkerboard.

43. *Suite of Stars* pin and earrings and *Super Heart* pin are by Elke Kuhn Moore. She is using applied sliced cane pieces on a checkerboard background. Note the use of the candy cane to finish the edge of the heart pin.

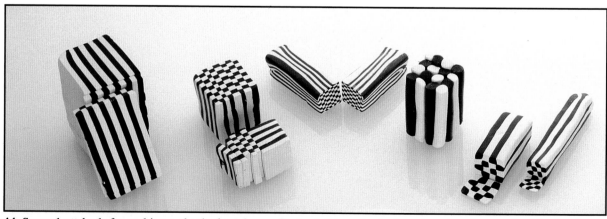

44. Several methods for making a checkerboard cane. To the left is a checkerboard made using a striped loaf and shifting the slices. On the right is a checkerboard made by packing a series of snakes into a loaf.

up like a checkerboard. For the second method, turn every other slice around to alternate the stripes. Be sure to match the pieces on both ends of the loaf. As described above, the loaf can be reduced, rolled into a log, or pressed into any other size you might want. It can be a component of another more elaborate loaf. Experiment. All sorts of interesting things will happen as you alter the shape of the loaf.

45. Four necklaces and a pin by Nan Roche made from geometric canes. The face pin is made in a loaf form.

Seminole Patchwork

The next variation I want to discuss is borrowed from the textile world - Seminole patchwork. It's a wonderful example of the possibilities for inspiration and imitation in this media. This is a method of piecing fabrics together to produce intricate geometric patterns and has been used by the Seminole Indians of Florida since the turn of the century.[5]

For this technique, start with a loaf of two colors with a black stripe running between them. Tip the block so that it is "looking up" at you. Slice off even slabs on the diagonal. Look at the diagram to guide you. Next, stagger these diagonal slabs in a regular pattern and press them together. Trim all faces of the block and you will find a zig-zag running through it. Basically you have taken one block, sliced it up and rearranged it into a new block. This technique can be used with blocks of stripes or any other patterns. You never know what might happen!

Traditional patchwork is another excellent source of ideas for block-like patterns. Look for books on patchwork patterns.

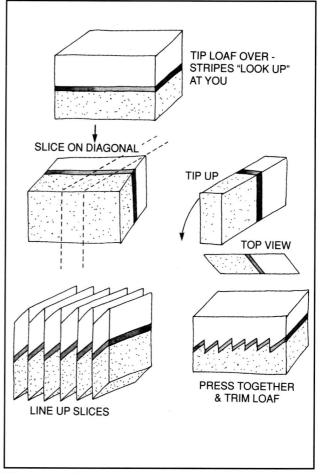

Illustration 43. Seminole Patchwork.

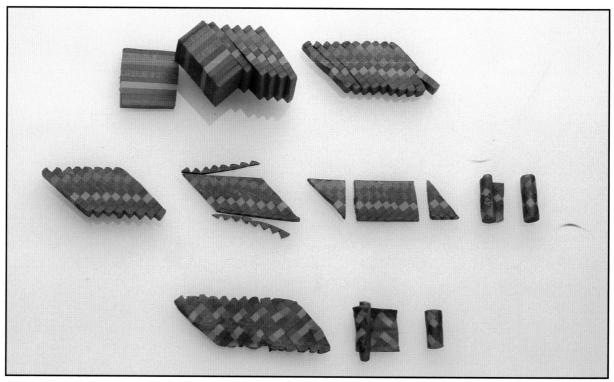

46. A demonstration of Seminole patchwork technique using a striped loaf.

Mokume Gane

This fascinating technique is borrowed from a Japanese metal working process. The word mokume means "wood grain" and gane means "metal," i.e. "wood grain metal." This technique will generate a pattern that looks like the annual growth rings of trees or the layers of crosscut wood.[6]

Start with a laminate of six to eight stripes using three colors. The stripes should be very fine, one to two millimeters, making a loaf about a centimeter high. There are two approaches to achieving a pattern with this method - excavation from the top or pressing up from below. It will be helpful to study the drawing before you begin.

The first method involves cutting away a canyon or hole from the top of the loaf. The excavated clay will reveal striped layers like rock strata. You can cut out troughs or holes of different sizes and shapes but don't cut all the way through. You must use a sharp gouge or knife to avoid smearing the layers as you cut. Now, flatten or roll the loaf down to a uniform thickness with the pasta machine or brayer and the underlying layers will be leveled up to the surface.

The other approach is rather opposite in concept. In this case, shapes are pushed up from underneath. Hold the loaf in one hand, turn it over and gently press a blunt tool like a pencil eraser or the blunt edge of a knife into the clay. It will leave a cavity on the back side and a raised bump on the surface. Using your blade, shave the block off to level it. This will reveal the underlying layers.

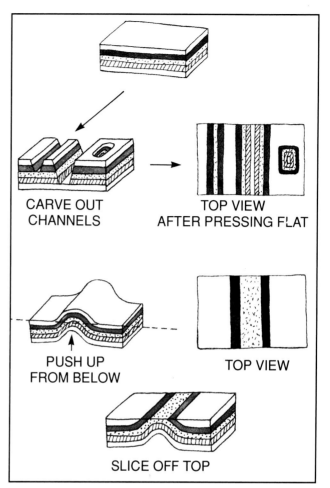

Illustration 44. Mokume Gane

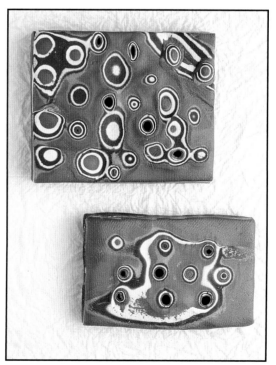

47. Two pins using the technique of Mokume Gane by Nan Roche.

TECHNIQUES WITH LOGS AND SHEETS

Wrapping

One of the easiest canes you can make is simply a log or snake wrapped with a sheet of clay. This elementary cane is a building block for many other more complex canes. It could be the pupil of an eye in a face cane, the center of a flower, or just an abstract design element.

To make this cane, roll out a log about the thickness of your thumb. Make a sheet of a different color. Lay the log on the sheet and check that it will wrap all the way around. When wrapping the log, you want the wrapping to meet but not to overlap which would create a thickening at this place. This meeting of ends is called a **butt joint** and there is an easy way to measure for it. Trim one edge of the sheet and roll the log in the sheet starting from this edge. Let the leading edge roll around and touch the other side of the sheet. This will leave a mark where you will trim the excess clay. When rolled, the two edges of the sheet should end in a butt joint meeting each other perfectly. If they don't quite meet you can pinch them together. Trim the excess clay off the ends and roll the log together.

You can add one or more layers, making a bull's-eye pattern. As shown before, using shaded layers can give an optical effect. Also think about varying the thickness of the wrappings for different effects. Wrapping various shapes will tend to protect them from being deformed during the rolling and will also separate shapes and patterns from one another. After wrapping, the log can be kept round or made into a square or any other shape by using your brayer.

As a variation, the central log could contain a pattern or the wrapping itself could be a pattern. A slice from a striped loaf could be used to wrap with in either direction. One direction will yield stripes running the length of the cane and the other will yield stripes running around the cane. The outside of the log may be decorated, and if the pattern runs the length of the log, it will add to the pattern of the cane. Any of the loaves that have been mastered before can be used as wrappings. Logs may also be wrapped with a multiple-layered sheet to add several layers with one wrap. Many combinations can be put together and built upon to make very complex loaves.

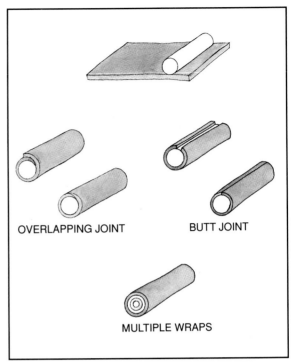

Illustration 45. Wrapping a Log.

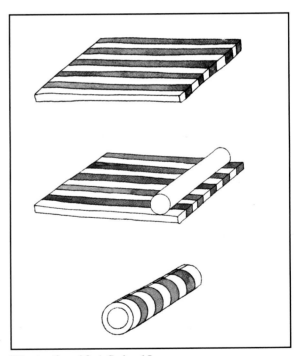

Illustration 46. A Striped Log.

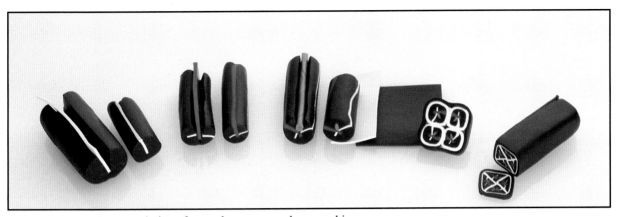

48. The slice and insert technique for random patterned canemaking.

Cut and Insert

This technique is very easy to do and produces very interesting, abstract effects. Once a cane has been made it can be reduced and reassembled to produce a secondary pattern that is even more exciting.

Start with a thumb-sized log of clay. Roll it evenly and trim the ends so you can see what you're doing. Slice the log lengthwise, as if it were a hotdog bun. Insert a sheet of clay into the opening and close the log back up, trimming off the excess sheet. Roll the log to fuse it together. You can cut and insert many times, rotating the log, overlapping the previous inlay. You can also inlay a small snake or other shape instead of a sheet.

Other Shapes

You can work with an infinite number of other shapes. Some of these shapes will be used when making complex figure canes. To make a piece of clay that is square use your brayer. Start with a ball of clay and roll it just a bit to begin to get a thick log. Then use the brayer to flatten it on one side. Rotate the log and flatten on the other side, making a square. You can use the brayer at an angle to get a wedge shape or triangular shape. These shapes can be cut into beads, or become elements of more complex canes.

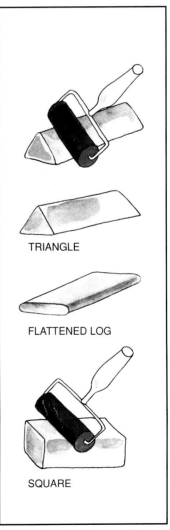

TRIANGLE

FLATTENED LOG

SQUARE

Illustration 47. Shaping Clay with a Brayer.

49. *Necklace of Angels* and *Icon Brooch* by Kathleen Dustin using thin slices of complex face and figure canes and simpler checkerboard and striped loaves.

The Complex Cane and Loaf

The term **cane** is borrowed from glassworking. It refers to a glass rod or cylinder that has a pattern running throughout the length. Near Venice, on the island of Murano, a glassworking technique using these canes became a high art. It was called millefiori which means "a thousand flowers." Canes were produced in molten glass in a large diameter and then, while molten, stretched down into small-diameter rods. This process is called "drawing" in the glass world. I call it **reduction** when applied to polymer clay. These glass canes with simple patterns, flowers or other images, were cut into pieces and applied to the surface of beads by melting in front of a hot torch or lamp, a technique called **lampworking**[7]. These techniques were used during the four hundred years of production of the beautiful Venetian trade beads that have traveled all over the world. The manufacture of glass canes is a fascinating and difficult process and was kept secret until modern times. But these same processes can be easily imitated with polymer clays. There are few other materials that can so beautifully and eas-

50. An assortment of face and pattern chips by Pier Voulkos. The box is not made of polymer clay.

ily express themselves using this technique. Elaborate patterns can be built up, the borders between colors remain distinct, and the cane can be cut and reassembled to create composite patterns. The possibilities for pattern formation can be extended beyond the limits of typical glassworking.

Simple Canes, Composite Canes and Loaves

While the canes made in glassworking are usually round, the word **cane** may also be used to refer to larger blocks of patterns, which I will call **loaves**. A loaf may be rolled into a round cane, or several canes can be assembled together into a loaf. Loaves need not be regular but can take on the shape of the image. I have already described many different simple canes and loaves in the previous sections. These simple patterns can be elaborated upon by reduction and recombination of simple canes and loaves of different patterns.

Composite canes are made by combining simpler canes to produce a more complex pattern. The elemental canes can be of the same pattern or different patterns. Loaves can be rolled into canes and will retain the internal pattern, though the outer surface will become distorted depending on the starting shapes. Canes and loaves can be combined or several different loaves can be

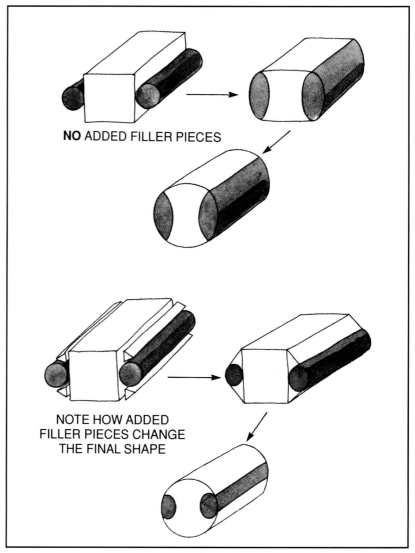

NO ADDED FILLER PIECES

NOTE HOW ADDED FILLER PIECES CHANGE THE FINAL SHAPE

Illustration 48. Loaf Assembly.

combined. A few tips on combining a round cane and a loaf: you can expect quite a bit of distortion in round canes when combining them with a flat loaf unless you pack some clay around the round cane. This will cushion the cane and prevent it from being flattened. You can also use a tool to impress a space into the loaf to accept the cane instead of building around it. You need to think ahead about the outcome of combining different shapes, and to manipulate them by adding clay where appropriate.

Reduction

Fundamental to the mechanism of making more complex canes is the process of reduction. It is through reducing and recombining simple canes that you will be able to make seemingly very elaborate and intricate patterns, very simply. This is your basic "something-for-nothing" technique!

If you haven't already discovered this effect, you're in for a real thrill. A good cane to use to demonstrate this technique is the simple wrapped cane. The pattern is most effective if you use highly contrasting colors. Roll a log about the thickness of your thumb and wrap it with a sheet of your second color. Next, roll the log down until it is pencil thick and about a foot long. Do this as evenly as possible. Remember, you will have better success if you use light quick, movements and pick your hand up off the clay while moving up and down the snake, pressing down the high spots. Don't worry if the ends are uneven, the pattern will be safe on the inside. Trim your ends and cut your snake into six equal pieces. Arrange the pieces in a group with a center and five pieces around it. Now, roll this grouping into a fat log until the borders of the pieces fuse into one cane. When you trim the ends you will see your first complex cane. But don't stop, continue reducing by rolling this new log down into a pencil-thick snake. Cut this snake into four equal pieces. Group these pieces and roll them together as before. This time when you trim the ends, the pattern is even more detailed. You can continue to do these reductions, but the pattern will become finer and finer until it disappears. Even very complex canes with irregular shapes can be reduced.

51. Reduction of complex canes. *Venus* by Kathleen Dustin showing different sizes of the same cane and a necklace with slices incorporated. *King and Queen* canes by Jamey D. Allen with reduced pieces in various shapes and two beads with the canes incorporated.

This ability to produce different sizes and shapes of the same pattern gives you an enormous range of design possibilities. Often a necklace will be much more interesting with a variety of shapes and sizes of beads using a common pattern to unify them. See the necklace by Sara Shriver on page 58 for a beautiful example of this.

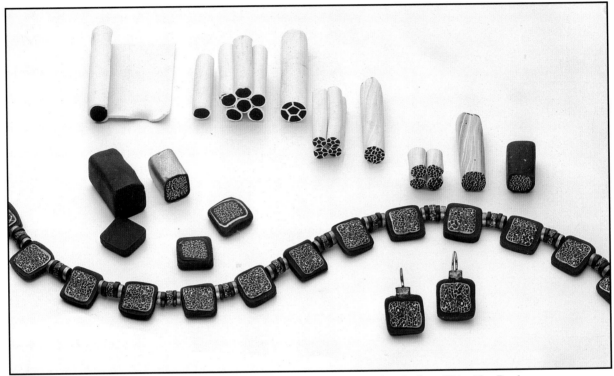

52. A lace cane. The steps in the process of making a lace cane are shown using Sculpey III by Nan Roche.

A Pattern Cane

Roll a cane of a light color, two inches long and 3/4" in diameter. Slice the whole cane in half lengthwise, like a hot dog bun. Insert a sheet of darker clay in between the two halves, trim the excess, reassemble, and roll the cane together. Turn the cane 90° and make another lengthwise slice, repeating the process. This should give you a cane with a cross in the middle. Even if the pattern isn't perfect, it will still be interesting. Go through one reduction as described above, arranging the pattern as shown in the drawing. The cane can be reduced and used as a surface decoration or shaped and sliced as beads.

Figure and Face Canes

Animals, faces, and even whole landscapes can be made as a cane or loaf. The process is the same as described above but requires a great deal more thought and planning. To make an irregular image that goes through the whole loaf (or cane), you need to think about the negative space around the figure as well as the shape of the figure itself. This takes a little practice in visualization. When designing a figure cane, it helps to draw it and think about it from the point of view of the simple elements that make it up. The ancient Egyptian and Roman glass mosaic pieces shown at the beginning of the book, are made in the same way, but of molten glass!

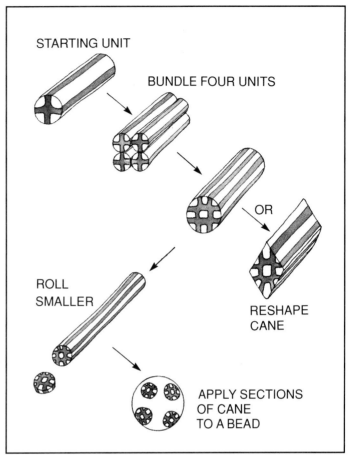

Illustration 49. A Pattern Cane.

TECHNIQUES FOR COMPLEX CANES

The Star

This five-pointed star is a fairly simple pattern, with all the points of the star being the same. You can make one cane with this image and assemble it into a star. All the clay will fuse when you roll the cane together, so make the center cane the same color as the points of the star. To make a white star with a black background, start with a solid black log. Cut an even slit through the middle without cutting all the way through. Now, roll a somewhat smaller snake out of white. Using your brayer, flatten it so that it forms a triangular wedge. Place this wedge into the cavity of the black and roll the unit together. Reduce it until you can cut it into five pieces. Roll a white snake that is about the same diameter as your other pieces.

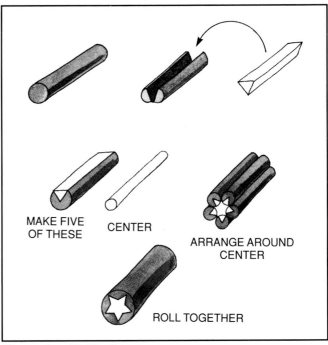

MAKE FIVE OF THESE   CENTER

ARRANGE AROUND CENTER

ROLL TOGETHER

Illustration 50. The Star.

Assemble the points of the star around the center snake. Make sure that you don't twist the units with the pattern in them. Match the white parts of the units so that no white shows when you assemble the cane. Roll the cane together and trim the ends. If your ends smear it may be because the clay is too warm. [This is especially a problem with Sculpey.] You can freeze the clay for 15 minutes or let the cane "rest" overnight before slicing.

The star can be reduced to a smaller size and used as a surface image on a background piece of clay. Many artists use this approach when making jewelry. Start with a flat sheet of clay for the background and then by arranging thin slices like snapshots on the surface, a complex scene may be built up. Remember that thicker slices will spread and distort. Making thin slices will also conserve your precious canes.

You may want to make a field of stars. This you can do by reducing your star cane and cutting it into regular lengths. In order to get a random effect you may want stars with some variation in sizes. Assemble your pieces together with some well-placed sheets of black to "randomize" them and press the loaf together. How about a moon or a cow?

Fish Scales

Fish scales are made in a different way and offer another approach to pattern making. Start with a wrapped log of two or three colors. Cut the log into thirds and assemble the loaf as shown in the illustration. The sections may not fit perfectly but will compress together into a scale pattern. Staggering and patching units together in this manner can be done in many ways. More ideas may be found in books for inspiration.

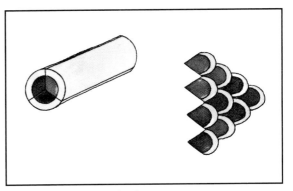

Illustration 51. Fish Scales.

53. *Mermaid Book* by Kathleen Amt. The dimensions are 4 x 6 inches. Notice the use of the fish scale cane for the mermaid's body. The printing is done by pressing alphabet rubber stamps into the wet clay, baking, and then filling the impressions with soft clay and rebaking. Notice the construction of the hinges. The book folds up like an accordion and fits into a book box. The photograph is by Marty Amt.

54. A selection of canes that are the elements of the *Mermaid Book* by Kathy Amt. The canes are made of Sculpey III. Photograph by Marty Amt.

The Flower

This pattern is one of Kathleen Dustin's. It is a stylized daisy, but almost any flower could be created using this technique. Flowers are good subjects. They have radial symmetry and learning to create them will improve your ability to visualize the making of more complex structures.

Start out by constructing the pieces that will be the petals. For this flower, the petals will have several layers of color. Roll a core snake. Next, prepare a larger log of color to do an asymmetrical wrap. Use your brayer to partially flatten the log, leaving it fairly thick. Pinch the edges so they taper and wrap it around your core, roll together. Prepare two more colors to make shading on the edges of the petals. Flatten them a little more than before and use a sheet that covers about half of the cane. Roll these in as well. Next, prepare a jellyroll cane for the center of the flower. Reduce your petal cane so that you can cut five equal pieces to go around the center. Choose a background color that will contrast with the flower and make some triangular wedges. These will separate and shape the petals. If you do not add them, the petals will fuse together.

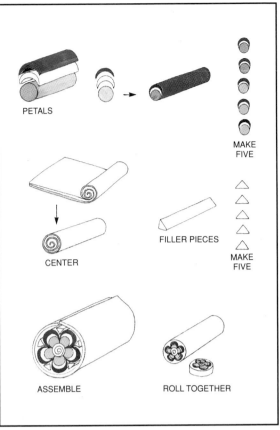

Illustration 52. The Flower.

For certain flower designs this might be desirable. Assemble the cane and roll it together. The top edges of the petals will still be showing. A final wrap in the background color will finish the pattern. As before, the flower cane can be reduced. In the photo, I have put small slices onto a base bead of the same color. The flowers appear to be floating on the finished bead.

55. A Flower Cane. The steps in the process of making a flower cane are shown using Sculpey III. The flower pattern is one of Kathleen Dustin's designs.

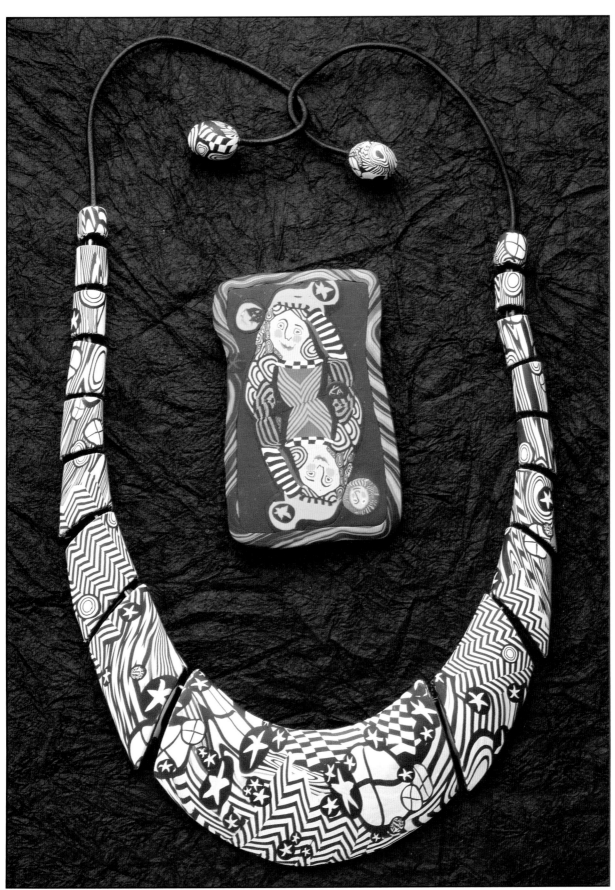

56. Necklace and pin by Kathleen Amt made with Sculpey III. The pin dimensions are 1.5 x 2.5 inches.

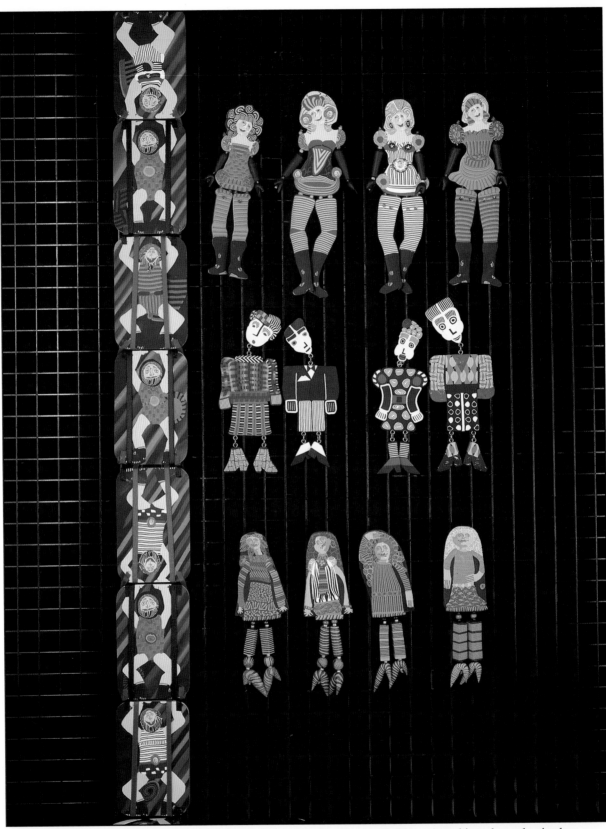

57. The movable people are: starting from the top, *Circus Ladies* pins by Kathleen Amt, hinged people pins by **Grove and Grove**, and *Friends* earrings by Kathleen Dustin. The Jacob's ladder toy, *Circus Acrobats*, is by Kathleen Amt. All are using canes and loaves for the figures. **Grove and Grove** work in Fimo and the other pieces are made of Sculpey III. An insert of Promat has been used in the Jacob's ladder for added strength. The pieces range in size from 3 to 5 inches.

The Face

Faces are more difficult to visualize because the elements that make a face - eyes, mouth, and nose - are relatively small in area compared to the flesh of the face. It's necessary to fill in these background areas in the correct proportions to get the correct proportions between the eyes, nose, and mouth. Faces are bilaterally symmetrical or mirror images of each side so the cane will be built a little differently than previous ones. Notice that some of the Roman glass face mosaics are made in half-faces. Two pieces were placed side-by-side to make a complete face.

This face pattern is also designed by Kathleen Dustin. When making a face, it is generally easiest to start

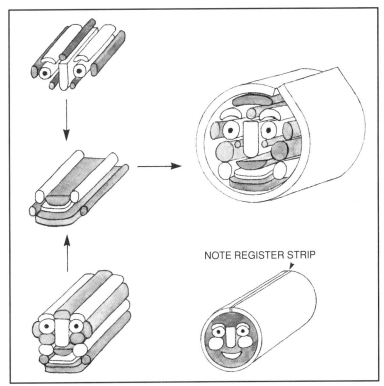

NOTE REGISTER STRIP

Illustration 53. A Face.

with the eyes and work into the surrounding structures. Study the illustration above first. Make the eye cane and cut it in half. Flatten a small log for eyebrows and cut it in two, the same length as the eye pieces. Prepare a slightly thicker wedge of lighter flesh color for the nose. The nose is the most prominent feature on the face and should be lighter to stand out from the image. Darker colors recede. Next make five pieces of flesh-colored clay for packing around the eyes, as shown. Press these pieces together slightly. Now, add on the lower part of the face. Make the cheek logs and a thin sheet for the mouth. Using the flesh color, make wedges of clay to go above and below the mouth and below the cheeks. Assemble these pieces as shown in the drawing and roll the cane together. Do a final wrap in the flesh color and roll together. You might want to give it hair or a hat and ears. This can be done by adding clay of various shapes and colors.

It is very helpful when making a pattern that has a specific orientation, like a face, to place a small strip of a different color along the top of the cane to serve as a register strip. Often, when rolling and reducing the cane, the pattern will begin to twist and the register strip will allow you to realign it.

When using Sculpey, it is also very important to let the cane rest for several days before reducing it. It may take several days to make a very complex cane and not all of the elements will be the same temperature when assembling. If some pieces are a lot softer, they will spread more than the surrounding clay and distort the face when you roll it.

Look back through the photos at some of the different faces that have been shown. Once you have developed several face canes, they can be used in many ways. Making faces in this way is not easy so don't get discouraged. If the face distorts or shifts, the expression is often much more interesting. So "hang loose" and just have some fun with it. Practice will improve each successive face.

Now, what can be done with them? Some artists like Kathleen Dustin and Kathleen Amt use their face canes along with other patterned canes to build a layered collage of thin slices on a surface piece of clay. This conserves the precious cane and allows great freedom of imagination, almost like painting a picture. The images can be very detailed. Because the clay will so readily fuse with itself, all trace of the borders between pieces of cane will disappear and the image appears as one. Look at the photos of Kathleen Dustin's necklace on page 74 and Kathleen Amt's necklace on page 83.

If you make your face cane large enough, it can be reduced and pieces of it can become a part of other more complex loaves. These composite canes can either be sliced very thin and placed on a backing or they may be sliced more thickly and used as is for earrings or pins. Look at the work of Grove and Grove, Kathleen Dustin, and Kathleen Amt in the photo on page 84. Notice how the pieces are hinged to make movable people.

58. A collection of complex canes by various artists. On the top row, from left to right: *Man in the Moon* pin of Sculpey III, 1", by Kathleen Amt; a face cane in Fimo by Marie Segal of **The Clay Factory**, *Rose Cane* by Jamey D. Allen, and *Whale* by Jamey D. Allen, both of Fimo. On the second row: *Sunflower* pin in Sculpey III by Kathleen Amt, *Eagle* in Fimo by Jamey D. Allen, *Night Duo* pin by Kathleen Amt, *Butterfly* cane in Fimo by Jamey D. Allen. In the third row: *Swallow* cane in Fimo by Jamey D. Allen, *Fish* cane in Fimo by Marie Segal, *African Woman* by Jamey D. Allen and *Howling Wolf* by Marie Segal of **The Clay Factory**. In the last row: *Snake and Jester* by Marie Segal, *Wolfman* by Jamey D. Allen and finally *Headhunter* cane by Marie Segal.

A Signature Cane

We have looked at some examples of patterns and images in caneworking, but letters and numbers can also be done. Many artists make a signature cane and use a small slice of it somewhere on their jewelry as a signature. The "signature" could be a logo or some other design combined with letters. Most letters can be constructed from sheets and wrapped logs. Letters can be cursive or block-like, block letters being easier to construct. The illustration shows one approach to making the letters "NR."

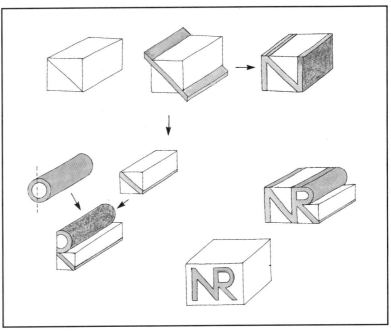

Illustration 54. A Signature Cane.

59. Four caneworked pins in Fimo by **Grove and Grove**. The three black and white cats measure 3" across.

60. Surface Design. In the upper left hand corner is a selection of glitters and metallic powders. In the upper right hand corner moving down to the left is a piece of clay with metallic foil that has been rolled through the pasta machine, next, impressions made with leather stamping tools dipped in metal powders followed by the same impressions after rolling through the pasta machine. The small square is made with a round metal tool dipped in metallic powder. The final pieces are examples of texturing and impressions using dental tools, sandpaper and other textures.

Surface Treatments

While the emphasis so far has been on caneworking, there is an equally exciting and relatively unexplored area in surface treatments. You can borrow ideas from metalworking, ceramics and the fiber arts as well as your local museum. The possibilities are endless. Sheets of clay can be textured and cut into shapes that can be overlapped to make earrings or necklace elements. Try using cookie cutters or canape cutters for shapes. Beads can be rolled on a textured surface. The clay can be textured using fabrics, natural objects like leaves or pine cones, wood, plastic, baskets, or a piece of metal stamped with a design. It can be scored with a stylus or pen nib or any other handy tool. This is called **chasing**. It can be painted or rolled in metal powders or foils. It can be used to take a transfer from newsprint or from a drawing done on tissue paper. You can use rubber or metal stamps, or metal type face, to put images onto the clay. You can take impressions and make molds. Let your imagination run wild. Ransack your house - objects in every room will have potential.

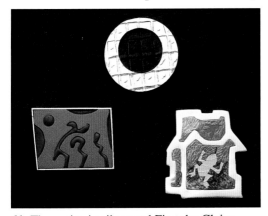

61. Three pins in silver and Fimo by Claire Laties. On the top is *Dot Box Brooch*, which measures two inches across. To the left is *Red and Blue Abstract Brooch*, the red is a piece of formica laminate that has been pierced with the blue Fimo extruded through and cased in a silver box. To the right is *Frog and Fly Brooch*, with the frog and fly made of formica laminate and the textured background of Fimo.

Texture

Texture is everywhere in our world. A few ideas for texture were just mentioned. Consider texture as a design element in jewelry. How and why you use it will make the difference between "ho-hum" and "wow". Think in terms of contrast, just as we did for color. Contrast of anything - texture, color or shape - provides a lot of excitement and movement in a piece of jewelry. The contrast can be extreme - glassy smooth and rough bark, or more subtle. Look around your environment at the textures you find interesting: shiny silk next to dull linen, an apple next to an orange or banana. Glossy magazine ads often have a lot of ideas in them for texture and color. If you like what you see, use it! Experiment with things you find in your house and make up some test pieces for future reference.

Use some basic design ideas along with texture. If you use an obvious grid pattern, like window screening to texture part of a piece, try repeating the grid design in a larger form elsewhere on the piece. Since the grid texture is square, use it along with round shapes for more excitement. Or use different sources of square texturing together, like fine screening and coarse screening together with coarse linen and hand scored square grating.

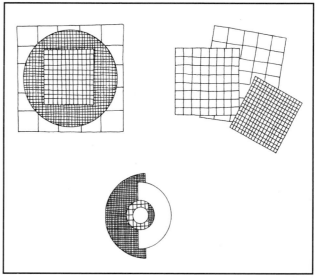

This idea is used very effectively in one of the pins by Claire Laties on page 89. If you use a texture with a predominant grain, turn the grain in the opposite direction in some part of the piece. Think of music. A repetition of beat with a variation on a melodic theme is very pleasing. Repetition and variation on a theme equals contrast with continuity and much more visual excitement. That's what it is all about in jewelry design. How to pack a lot of visual impact into a small space.

Illustration 55. Texture.

Texture can be used to help produce a convincing imitation, like using wood for wood grain or making an impression of leaves. Nature is a excellent source of things with which to make textures. Pine cones and seed pods, bark, and shells are all wonderful tools for texture.

Fabrics are wonderful for imitation since the clay can be shaped so much like fabric when it is thin. Leather, woven baskets, textured papers or crinkled up paper, a ball of string, corrugated cardboard on end, sandpaper, burlap, netting, and stiff bristled brushes are just a few things that come to mind from the textile world.

Textures can also come from our technological world. Think of all the stamped and textured plastic parts and coverings in our environment - phonographic records, styrofoam, pot scrubbers, combs, bubble packing, plastic wrap (crinkled up) and onion bags. Many kitchen items offer interesting textures as well - graters and strainers, a square skewer can be rolled across the clay, slotted spoons, not to mention patterned dishes and flatware. Cut crystal and your mothers spoon collection, or that pewter cup with the stamped pattern, your silver service, etc., are all worthy of investigation. Remember to clean the items carefully before using them again with food. Hardware items might include springs, rolled across the clay, nuts and bolts, textured metal handles on socket wrenches, screening and netting, saw blades and many other items. You might also think of your own hands as a texturing tool, or your dog's nose.

Chasing

Another approach to texturing is to use chasing. Chasing is a word that comes from metalworking. It sounds fancy, but all it refers to is incised carving. Almost anything can be used to carve with, from something as simple as a tooth pick or a nail to jeweler's wax carving tools or dental picks. Ask your dentist for old dental tools. A single tool can be used to produce many different marks and textures. Look at the illustration on page 17.

62. Three pins by Patricia Kutza of **What Knot.** The cobalt blue ultrasuede series is made of textured polymer clay with ultrasuede fabric and mirror inserts.

Stamping

Stamping is really an elaborate variation of chasing. Instead of using a simple tool to impress a pattern into the clay, you use a more complicated "ready-made" design to stamp the clay. Stamps of your own designs can be made by carving rubber erasers. Carved wood, or a piece of linoleum glued onto wood and carved, will also work well. Of course, rubber stamps can be purchased with all kinds of wonderful designs already on them. Drawings or images of your own can be made into stamps by some commercial companies. Another great source of stamps are metal leather working tools. They can be obtained from leather working supply stores. You might also keep a look out for old printers' type at surplus and antique stores. Along these lines, look for old printing plates and other printing paraphernalia.

There are many different ways stamps can be used. The most direct approach is to simply stamp into the clay. Stamps can be used on top of a color or pattern design, much like quilting patterns are superimposed on top of piece work in a quilt. Stamps can be dipped into metallic powders, colored chalk, or paints and applied to the clay. The color ends up in the valleys created by the stamp and delineates the pattern very clearly. Designs can be repeated in arrays or they can be shifted slightly to give a shadow effect. The design will be spread and elongated if you subsequently run the clay back through the pasta machine after stamping.

Another interesting variation that highlights the design is to stamp an impression into the clay and then bake the stamped clay. After cooling, fill the impression with clay of a different color and then re-bake the piece. Be sure to let the piece cool completely before filling the impression with unbaked clay. Use a dental pick or a

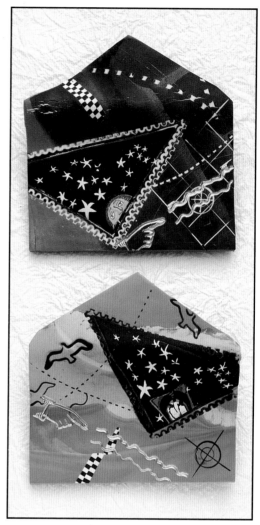

63. Two map pins by Kathleen Amt. The pins were made using cane slices and the inlay technique of making an impression, baking and then filling the impression with clay and rebaking. The gold is applied using a hot press and gold foil. The pins are 2.5 inches in diameter.

small flexible metal rib to scrape away any residual clay from the impression. Do a final cleaning with alcohol before the second baking. A freeform design or other texture could also be filled in this way. Kathy Amt has made beautiful use of this technique in her books by using printers' type to create words and rubber stamps for images. Look at her work on page 119, the Mermaid book on page 81 and the map pins on this page where she uses tracing wheels and leather tools to create the design.

Surface Materials

Another way to decorate the surface of the clay is to use any of a variety of paints, metallic powders and glitters. These substances can be dusted on, painted on with brushes, or stamped on with stamps.

Paints

The most compatible paint to use is acrylic paint. It can be painted on before or after baking and doesn't suffer from the heat. Other water based paints like watercolors and temperas should be experimented with; because they are in a water base instead of a plastic base like acrylic paints they may not stick to the clay very well. Oil paints and printers' inks should be tested before using, as there may be solvents in the paints that soften the clay after baking.

Tee-shirt paints or puff paints are now popular and available in most art supply stores and craft stores. They are wonderful to work with because they come in many colors and textures. Some are shiny, some flocked, and some have glitter in them. They are similar to acrylics but a little thicker and will form a raised bead on the surface of the clay. They are slightly rubbery when they dry but hold up well to baking.

Glitters and Powders

While browsing at the art supply store you may find a number of other surface treatments such as metallic powders, glitters, charcoal chalk, and thermography powders. Thermography powders are used for embossing. Ink is applied to the surface of paper and, while still wet, the powder is dusted into the wet ink. The paper is then heated to melt the thermography powder creating a raised surface on the paper. Metallic powders are used for gold leafing or to mix with paints and may be found in the framing section or paint section. See the appendix for sources. You can also experiment with powdered charcoal, powdered chalk, and powdered makeups.

Metallic powders come in two types: finely ground metal powders and mica powders, also called interference pigments. The metal powders are made of aluminum, copper or bronze metals and they should be handled wearing a mask; they are not healthy to breathe. I recommend using gloves and most importantly, a dust mask, when working with any of these powders and carefully disposing of the residue. They can be easily used by dipping a small amount out of the bottle onto a large piece of wax paper. After using, the paper can be folded up and thrown away. The manufacturers also add a word of caution about the aluminum based powder. Aluminum can be explosive if enough is present in the air, although it would require at least an ounce in suspension in an average sized room to cause problems. Definitely keep these powders away from small children and pets and supervise older children carefully.

The mica based powders are less hazardous because they are not directly toxic, but they are also not healthy to breathe. They are usually harder to find in powder form but can be ordered by mail. Papermakers add these powders to their paper pulp to make iridescent papers. They may also be called interference pigments and are used in makeups and other cosmetics. Brush on eyeshadows and cosmetic powders may also be used, but experiment first. Lois Brandt used these powders on her wall sculpture on page 122 (photo 95).

Colored chalks may also be used by rubbing them onto a piece of paper and either using your finger or a brush to apply them to the clay.

Metal Foils

Metal foils, such as gold and silver leaf, are also possible materials to use for surface decoration. Gold and silver leaf consists of very thin sheets of metal foil in a booklet used for surfacing wooden frames or other objects. The foils come in a package with the leaf sandwiched between sheets of tissue paper. The leaf is so thin it will blow away if you are not careful. You can usually purchase it at art supply stores. It comes in 24K gold and sterling silver which are expensive, or in copper and aluminum sheets with are inexpensive.

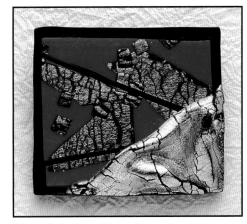

64. A pin by Kaz Yamashita using fractured gold foil pieces on-laid and folded like fabric. The pin measures 2.5 inches.

Foils may be pushed through a strainer with an old tooth brush to create metal flecks. Gently press the flecks into the surface of the clay before baking. The foil may be used simply by applying a sheet or piece onto the unbaked clay. It will stand up to baking very well. An interesting effect will be produced if the foil is fractured on the surface of the clay. This is easily done by rolling the foiled clay through the pasta machine. The foil will fracture into a pattern on the clay surface. If you further reduce the thickness setting on the pasta machine and roll the foiled clay through again, it will fracture even more. The clay can be folded into a design or pieces can be cut and laid onto other designs. Look at the broaches of Kaz Yamashita on page 54 and on this page. If left uncoated, these foils will tarnish in time.

Transfers

Another wonderful possibility for design with the clay is to make transfers. The clay is sticky and will pick up images from newsprint and from drawings done on tissue paper.

To make a transfer from tissue paper, you may use a wide variety of pencils and crayons. Colored charcoal pencils work very well, as do Cray-pas, Nupastels, and oil pastels.[8] Your drawing should be done on a good quality tissue paper. You can use shading and blending of colors to achieve a feeling of depth in the drawing. The tissue paper image is then inverted onto a sheet of clay and gently rubbed with the fingers to transfer the image. It can be left on the clay overnight and the transfer will be even more complete.

65. A series of transfers from newsprint onto clay.

Once the image is on the clay, it can be trimmed to size or pieces of it used as a collage element on another object. After baking, the image seems to be permanent and does not rub off, but I would recommend coating it with matte lacquer just to be on the safe side.

The other transfer technique involves using newsprint. Black and white images are the strongest with recently printed newsprint working best. Some newspapers will not work at all. This may be due to the ink formulation used in printing. Select the image and cut it out. Invert it onto the clay and leave it overnight. The paper will become soaked with the oily plasticizer and appear transparent.

Gently peel off the paper and you'll have your image. Glossy color ads do not work at all. Color newsprinting will work to some extent but the image is very faint. Try experimenting - some printers may use inks that will transfer. Some types of copier inks will also transfer.

66. A transfer of colored chalk pencil lines from paper onto clay.

Another idea for transferring is to take a rubbing from either a raised or indented pattern using charcoal pencils or pastels and then to transfer it onto the clay. You should pay attention to the base color of the clay and the colors used to transfer to obtain a nice effect.

Monotype prints can be made from a glass plate in the same way. One idea is to add some raised texture onto the plate with an acrylic gel medium or silicone gel, and then to draw on the plate and pull an image off it with a sheet of clay. The raised pattern will be an indented pattern when printed. Think of the clay as a piece of paper and the plate as a print block. A piece of linoleum or formica could also be used in this way.

67. A scarab necklace by Helen Banes using mold making techniques. Also shown is a mold and the scarab that made it.

Molding

Molding is another marvelous technique, ripe with possibilities. There are many different things from which to make molds and many ways to use them. A simple way to start is to make a mold of a cameo or scarab. Start with a kneaded wad of clay. Rub a thin layer of mineral oil on the object and press it into the clay. You can bake the two together or gently pull the object out and then bake the clay mold by itself. If you bake them together, be sure that the mold-making object will withstand the heat. You now have a mold that you can use to replicate your original object. To do this, coat the baked mold with a tiny amount of mineral oil and press some kneaded clay into it. Talcum powder and water may also be used to prevent sticking. Again, you may bake the two together if the mold is deep, or pull them apart if the mold is shallow and then bake only the cast piece. When making a mold you must be careful that the mold has no under cuts or the two will lock together with baking. See the work of Wayne Farra, Helen Banes and Ingrid Stark.

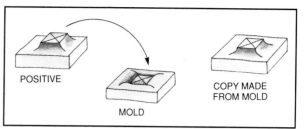

Illustration 56. Mold Making.

68. A *Celtic Pectoral* made of Sculpey III by Ingrid Frances Stark. The piece is made from a mold that has been incised with the Celtic pattern. A new piece is transferred from the mold. The piece is then painted with acrylic paints after baking. The pectoral measures 5" across.

69. Two necklaces, a bracelet and two pins by Wayne Farra of **Studio One-of-a- Kind**. Only the type face impressions are of polymer clay. A mold is made from a printers plate and baked. Raw clay is pressed into the mold and baked. Talcum powder is dusted on the clay to give the appearance of slate. The beads are strung onto rubber gasket material.

70. *Robin Refuse*, a collage sculpture by Jo Ellen Trilling, uses bones, glass, rubber wheels and metal in conjunction with polymer clay. The two pins are titled *Mona Balona* and *Van Gogh's Ear* by Joe Lee. The pictures are painted on stiff paper with pen and ink and the ear and Mona's tongue are made of polymer clay.

Collage

Collage refers to an art technique that makes use of various materials, not normally associated with one another, together in one piece. Often the term is associated with drawings or paintings that use newsprint, found papers and other objects, together with paint and pencil on a flat surface. Collage can also refer to three-dimensional objects and sculpture made out of found materials and other "junk."

There are very few other collage media that possess as much versatility as polymer clay. Almost any color can be mixed from the clay, it will not shrink or change color when baked, and the baking temperatures are low enough to allow almost any material to be included while baking. The clay can be also be drilled, filed, and cut after baking. It can be pushed together like tinkertoys, screwed and riveted together, or glued. It can be textured, painted on or stamped into. It imitates anything opaque. It really is the ultimate collage material.

The list of possible collage materials is almost endless, but I will cite some basic categories to serve as inspiration. The criteria for collage materials are that they be able to withstand the 270°F baking temperature, that they not be perishable with time, and that they have some interesting color, shape or meaning. The following are some ideas for materials.

In the area of glass, think about using beads, old lenses, chips of worn beach glass, jewels from the craft store, old buttons, mirrors, prisms, dolls eyes, diffraction grating and watch parts and faces. Surplus and scientific supply catalogs are a great source.

Ceramics might include broken pottery shards from the junk yard or beach, small insulators, and beads.

Metals might include springs, rusty pieces of steel, electronic parts like diodes and resistors, cast jewelry parts, pins and needles, wire of different sizes and metal types, old coins, small chains, shavings from tooling machines, and other weird little parts of unknown origin.

Natural materials include seeds, seed pods, and dried leaves, pieces of bark like birch bark and palm raffia, leathers and other animal skins, shells, gems and minerals, crystals, natural colored sands, beetle wings and carpels, feathers, teeth, fossils, pieces of bone, and wood.

Miscellaneous man-made materials are also worthy of collage. Paper is a big category including candy wrappers, foils, stamps, colored acetate, Japanese papers and handmade papers, newsprint, magazine glossies, photos, bubble wrap, film strips, ticket stubs, shopping bags, and cardboard. Other man-made materials might include parts of old toys, wheels, bicycle reflectors, game pieces, and a myriad of other "found" objects.

The fiber world yields another set of great collage items - wool, silk or cotton yarns and cords. Look in your local knitting shop. Fabrics from coarse to very fine weaves can be used as well as brocades with a pattern woven into the cloth. Canvas, muslin, cotton sheeting, coarse to fine linen, silks, ribbons, cording, braids, baskets, and many other things can be used. Your sewing store will suddenly become ripe with potential as will every other aspect of your life. The world around you will become a perpetual beach to comb for special objects for collage. You now have an excuse for saving that pretty piece of paper or interesting button that you dug up in the garden. If you're into "something for nothing" or recycling, then collage will be inherently satisfying. Some people call it the magpie syndrome. I should know.

71. Four stamp pins by Tory Hughes. The artist uses found objects, metal wire and stamps in her compositions. The stamps are lacquered after baking to protect the paper.

There is a lot that goes into combining diverse materials effectively. Just sticking random things together can often appear chaotic and uninteresting. In a good collage, every object is there for a reason, either because of its shape or color or because of the content of its meaning. Collages are often evocative of a mood or complex set of ideas without explicitly representing them. The idea of using subtle references are what make collages so compelling. Of course, good design and use of color is also necessary. Two of my favorite collage artists are Joseph Cornell and Kurt Schwitters. You may want to look in your local library for books about these artists and others like Pablo Picasso and Robert Rauschenberg.

72. A collage titled *Shrine: Earth Egg* by Wilcke H. Smith. The piece measures 11" x 14" and is made of amaté paper, horsetail reed, porcupine quill, and ostrich eggshell discs with the central figure in polymer clay.

Collage Assembly

There are a few tips for assembly that will be useful to keep in mind. Objects that are embedded in the clay will not stay there unless they are held in place with a small overlap of clay. Where this is not possible, simply press the object onto the clay and leave its impression. After baking, you can glue it in place.

A wide variety of glues may be used with polymer clay, depending on the application. The gel form of superglue is a popular type, but epoxy, silicone glue and hot melt glue will also work. All glues should be tested. Individual brands may have solvents in them that will dissolve the clay. Any plastic objects should be tested before you use them in your collage - they may melt. Feathers and hair should be glued in place after baking. Papers, metal powders and foils, and other surface objects that are thin and may rub off should be coated with a lacquer. Not all lacquers are compatible with polymer clay and some may soften the clay even after baking. The best lacquer to use is made by the Fimo company, Eberhard Faber. Any other coatings should be tested before using. Do not use nail polish. Acrylic gel medium for thinning acrylic paints will also work well but is not as transparent as the Fimo lacquer.

73. The *Sea Fantasy* necklace and earrings are by Jane van der Kuil and made of Sculpey III, abalone shells, freshwater pearls, starfish, bronze powder and a sea horse. The piece is 3.5" across.

Metal wires or rods that are pushed into the clay may pull out after baking if they are perfectly straight; textured or scored wires will have less tendency to do this. This may only be a problem if the metal piece will be taking some stress like an ear wire for an earring or a hinge or pendant hook. In this case the wire should be kinked a bit before embedding and will be less likely to pull out. If you are worried, you may also use a dab of glue around the wire.

There are many ways to hinge or join unrelated objects. This will require some imagination and innovation on your part, depending on the problem at hand. You will find that you begin to notice these details of design as you face construction problems of your own. Sometimes the solution will come from the most unexpected places. All of this is part of the art of collage.

74. The necklace and pin are by Tory Hughes. Tory has used Fimo with metal and ceramic scarabs, beetle wing carpels, and small fishing weights in the necklace and a stamp and bent metal wire in the pin.

75. These wonderful *Wee Folk* are created by Maureen Carlson using Fimo mixed with Sculpey. *Phyllis Jane, the Storykeeper Doll*, is about 10" tall while seated. Her body is stuffed and her arms, legs and head made of polymer clay. The four characters on the right are members of a chess set titled *The Shadow People vs. The Pretenders.*

Sculpture

There are many different forms of sculpture to be found in our world, from representational figures to abstract monoliths, buildings, furniture, pottery, jewelry, and even stoneworks like Stonehenge and the wrapped buildings of the artist, Cristo. The two most basic and ancient uses of sculpture were to render the human form and to make vessels. One is a more spiritual use of sculpture and the other more functional. The earliest sculptures found go back over 30,000 years. The essential joy of molding clay into something meaningful is a very ancient feeling. Try to connect with that feeling and use everything you see around you for inspiration.

76. The pin is *Louise* by Jeffrey A. Kyle and is 2.5" tall. The pearl posts are detachable and may be worn separately.

Now imagine all of the previous techniques you've learned applied to three-dimensional forms! Because the clay doesn't dry out and requires little technical knowledge, experimentation and imagination can run wild. The following techniques described are only to serve as guidelines for you to start your own exploration.

The Human Form

There are several basic approaches that artists have used for sculpting the human form. One approach has already been touched upon in the previous chapter, that of complex caneworking. Although it really is flatworking and the face or image is sliced into flat pieces, I'm including it in this chapter because these flat pieces can be treated in a sculptural way by hinging the figures and making puppets or toys. Another approach is to sculpt cameos or faces as bas-relief with one surface flat and the image emerging from it. And finally there is full three-dimensional dollmaking. The polymer clays have been used for many years by dollmakers and puppetmakers as well as by miniaturists, dollhouse collectors, and model railroad enthusiasts. I will discuss each of these approaches only briefly and let the artists' works speak for themselves as inspiration for you to try your own.

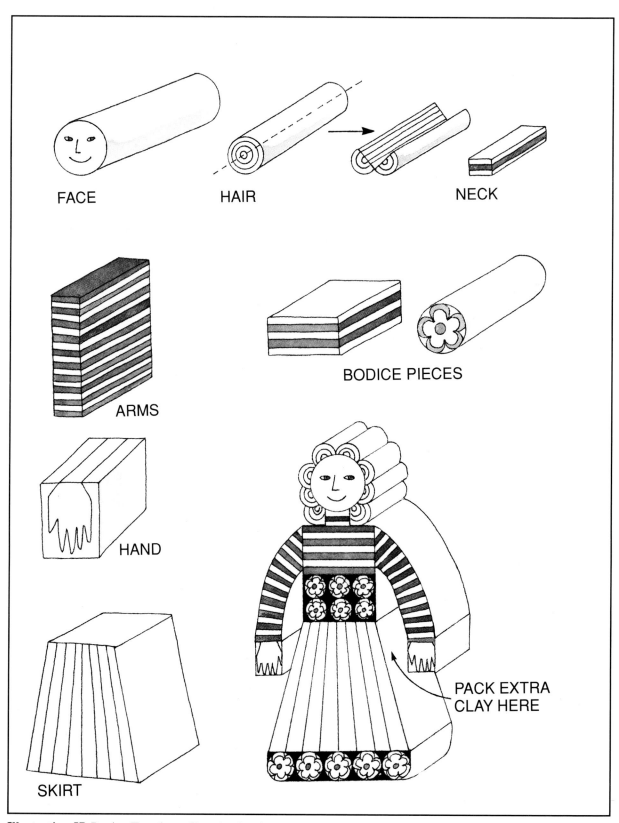

FACE

HAIR

NECK

ARMS

BODICE PIECES

HAND

SKIRT

PACK EXTRA
CLAY HERE

Illustration 57. Putting Together a Complex Loaf.

Caneworking, Building Figures, and Hinging

Refer back to the section on complex caneworking for ideas on how to make elaborate figures in canes. This is an acquired skill that is built upon over time so don't get discouraged. Start simply and gradually add more and more elements to your loaves. Using complex loaves that represent various elements of a human figure, you can put together movable dolls or puppets by hinging them together. Drawing #58 on this page shows one way in which this hinging can be done, though there are many other ways to do it. Some artists use nylon fishing line or thread and feed it through pierced holes and knot it. Others use small metal hinges. Try out some different techniques.

Start by rolling out a sheet of solid colored backing clay. Cut out a shape that will be the same size as your canes. Next, using a small length of wire about one inch long, bend it into a small loop that is slightly opened at one end. Bend some kinks in the straight part of the wire to prevent the wire from pulling out of the clay after it is baked. Lay the wire pieces on the backing clay with the loops positioned properly and place a slice of your figure cane on top. Gently press the two together so that the wire is embedded between the two pieces. Repeat the process for the other elements and bake all the pieces. When cool, interlock the metal loops and close them with a jewelers pliers. The use of silver wire will add elegance.

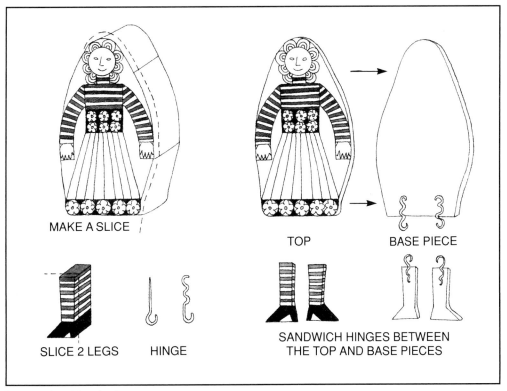

Illustration 58. Hinging.

Bas-Relief

Bas-relief is another sculpting technique in which the figure projects slightly from the background. See the cameo pin by Jeanne Sturdevant on page 55 (photo 32) and the pin by Jeffrey Kyle on page 103. In this technique, clay is pressed onto a backing and then molded into shape with the fingers and sculpting tools. Once a face shape is roughed out, the tools can be used to carve the details of the face. Small bits of other colors of clay can be shaped and pressed into place for lips or eyes. Textures can be added for hair or eyelashes. Paints, fabrics and collage materials can also be added.

77. These three show pins are by Diane Plumley and pertain to her background as an actress. The puppets stand 3" to 4" high and are *The Beast*, from **Beauty and the Beast**, *The Queen of Hearts*, from **Alice in Wonderland**, and *Marvin the Magnificent Magician*. She uses brocades and lamé fabrics to dress the puppets and feathers and fur for the hair.

78. This sculpture is called *Dog's Skeleton* by Doug Kennedy and is part of a work in progress. The skeleton is built around a wire armature and measures 8" x 10". It is made of Fimo and Sculpey and will be an element in a shadow box collage.

Three-Dimensional Sculpture

Three-Dimensional sculpture is the last technique I'm going to discuss. Working in three dimensions is a bit more challenging than working in two because you have to pay attention to all sides of an image. But don't be discouraged, this clay is perfect with which to experiment. Unlike ceramics, it doesn't dry out and is easy to mold or carve. You can play around with it until the image is just right and then bake it. When doing sculpture, good powers of observation come in handy and having a model of what you want to sculpt will help, but freeform sculpting is also fun. Don't let yourself be intimidated by the word "sculpture" - experiment and have fun.

79. This chess set of 32 pieces is titled *The Shadow People vs. The Pretenders* by Maureen Carlson. Each figure has his or her own character and personality. The tallest figures stand 9" high and are made of Fimo with Super Sculpey added to soften it. The chess set tells a story of conflict between people who are always "on stage" (the mask wearers) and those who let their inner passions and emotions show.

Armatures

Most artists use an armature to start a clay sculpture. An armature is a scaffolding around which the clay will be wrapped, leaving the center of the piece more or less hollow. For ceramics this is important because a solid block of ceramic clay could split or blow up in the kiln if it is fired too fast for the water to be released. Though this is not a problem with polymer clay, the use of an armature saves clay and makes the sculpture sturdier and lighter in weight. The armature can be made of wire, wood, wadded aluminum foil or any other material that can stand the 270°F heat of baking - even stiff poster board. Some dollmakers use aluminum foil that has been covered with masking tape to start a dolls head. Often the armature itself is important for attaching one part of the sculpture to another, like the head to the body. If the sculpture is small you may not need to use anything more than a toothpick or popsickle stick to hold the head onto the body. Dollmakers have developed many methods for doing this which I will not describe here. Several publications that discuss these techniques are listed in the bibliography.

People-making

Maureen Carlson, whose work starts off this chapter, has produced several wonderful videotapes on sculpting people. It is impossible to do this subject justice in this book and I highly recommend obtaining copies of the tapes if you are interested in doll making. See the listing in the bibliography for more information. I will give a brief and general description of her working techniques.

Maureen uses only a few simple tools - a toothpick or needletool, the head of a nail, a small kitchen knife, a blunt dowel, and a pasta machine to roll sheets. She makes the head first from a ball of clay. The eyeballs have been baked separately beforehand. The eye sockets and mouth are made by cutting a small slit in the clay, pushing the needletool in and gently rocking it back and forth to create a cavity. The eyeballs are pushed into the sockets and tiny pieces of clay are used to make the eyelids. A tongue or teeth may be placed in the mouth and the mouth shape formed into any expression.

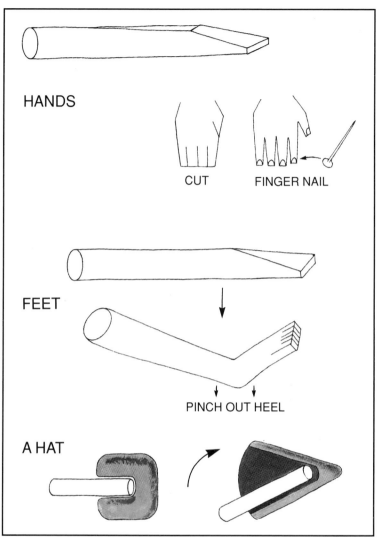

Illustration 59. Sculpting Little People.

Lips are added with colored clay. A toothpick is pushed into the base of the head and then the body is made. She starts with a fat cylinder of clay for the body and then "dresses" it with sheets of clay that have been textured with cloth. The pieces are cut, stretched and folded into place like fabric. Arms and legs are made out of cylinders of clay from which the hands and feet are formed as follows. Wedges of clay are shaped on the end of the arm from which the fingers are cut. Fingernails are made with the head of a nail by pressing down on the ends of the fingers. The foot is made in the same way except that the heel is pinched out of the cylinder and the cuts to make the toes are smaller. A hat is made by starting with a ball of clay into which a blunt dowel is pushed part of the way. Imagine juicing an orange. The dowel is rotated in the clay, making a larger and larger opening. Hold the clay stationary on the table and roll the dowel, as if it were a small rolling pin, without letting it pierce the cap. By pressing on the clay and rotating the dowel, a hollow cone shape is produced which makes a wonderful hat. Finally, the head is pressed onto the finished body and the neck is joined to the body and smoothed together. The hair is added and finally the hat. Hair is make by slicing a sheet of clay into tiny strips. The individual strips can be twisted to look curly or left straight. Study the drawing to help you visualize these techniques.

Stuffed Dolls

Another approach to dollmaking is to make the head, arms and legs out of clay and make the body out of fabric. Look at the work of Maureen Carlson on page 102 and Deborah Banyas on page 48 and below. Limbs and heads can be attached by forming a lip on the clay piece around which fabric can be gathered.

Any other subject can also be sculpted. The pieces may be used in collage as in the box of Douglas Kennedy on page 110 (photo 81). Fantasy, humor or more serious themes may be explored.

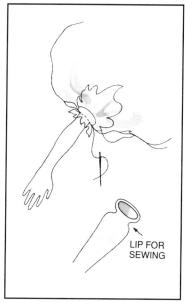

Illustration 60. Attaching a Doll's Arm

80. These two sculptures, *Cat and Mermaid* are by Debra Banyas. The arms, legs and heads are of polymer clay. They measure 10" tall.

81. This collage is by Doug Kennedy and is titled *Autumnal Spirit*. The piece measures 7" x 9". It is in a wooden box and is sculpted of Fimo and Super Sculpey some of which is painted. The eyes are glass.

82. This *Periodical Cicada* is by Jane van der Kuil. It is made of Sculpey, wire, acrylic paint and fabric. It measures 3" across in wing span.

83. This small red and blue kaleidoscope necklace is made by Alice and Willie Stevenson of **Spirit Scopes**. The clay is built around a tube that contains the mirrors. It measures 4" in length.

84. A necklace and two pins by Janice Farley, titled *Flower Box* and *Flower Pot*. The necklace is fancifully titled *Sandwiched*.

85. The *Christmas Tree Light Bulb* necklace and earrings are made by Marie Segal of **The Clay Factory**, from Fimo. The bulbs measure 1 1/4 " in length.

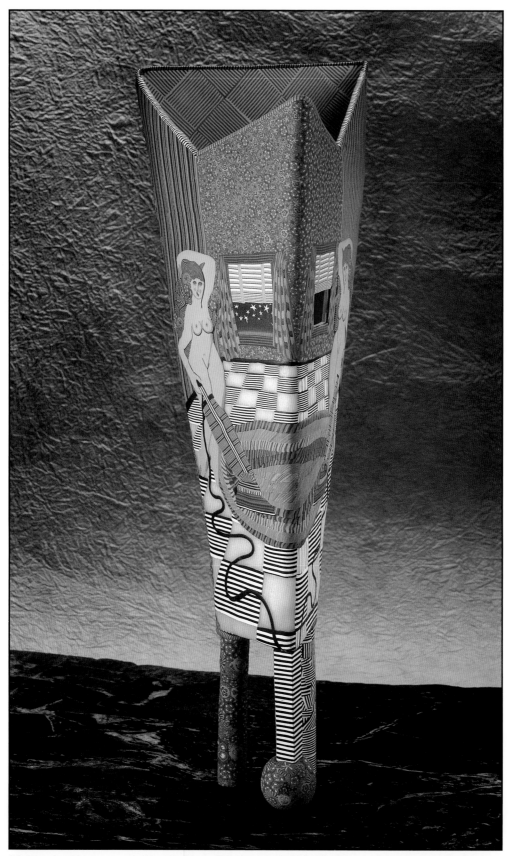

86. *Vacuum Venus*, a vessel by Kathleen Dustin, stands 12" tall. She used transparent Sculpey to achieve areas in the vessel where light comes through. The piece is built up of slices of complex canes built up on a slab foundation of clay.

Vessels

Ceramic vessels can be made in many different ways. The parallels with polymer clay are numerous with the exception of wheel throwing. Pottery and books on pottery will be a splendid source of inspiration. Slabs can be assembled into boxes, free-form pots, and many other shapes. Thinner flat sheets can be draped and wrapped around a form, or vessels can be made by the coiling method or the pinch pot method which I will describe.

Slabworking

Slabworking refers to a ceramic technique where slabs of clay are rolled out, cut into sheets, and then assembled into boxes, vases or other shapes. I will describe a very simple slab pot but an infinite variety of shapes can be made with slabs. Square vessels, triangular and round shapes, or free-form geometric shapes are all possible. Some of the shapes will be more difficult to engineer than others. Square shapes are difficult because of the precision needed for all the joints. To start, try the more freeform shapes with fewer joins. The slabs can be

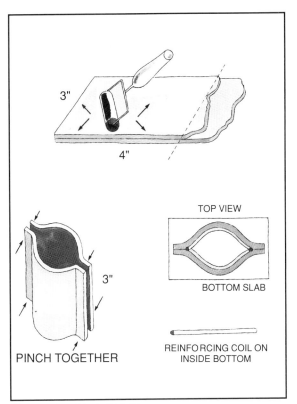

Illustration 61. A Slab Pot.

decorated with slices of patterned canes, pieces of colored clay, collage materials, dusted with metallic powders, painted, textured, pierced, stamped, etc., before assembling. Take a look at the photo on the preceeding page of Kathleen Dustins' vase, and the boxes made by Grove and Grove on page 116. These are both examples of slab work. The strength and precision of the joints in these pieces is very difficult to obtain. Start out with a simple piece first.

To make a simple slab pot, roll your slabs and decorate them as you wish. The slabs of clay need to be thick enough to withstand the vertical weight of the vessel. If you are using a pasta machine to roll the slabs, the #1 thickness setting on the machine may not produce slabs that are thick enough for larger vessels. Use two sheets and press them together for a thickness of about three mm. Using your brayer, start at one edge and roll the pieces together pressing out the air bubbles as you go. You may want to use the stronger clays like Promat and Fimo, or a mixture of clays, for one of the layers. Make two 3" x 4" slabs and one slab large enough to be the bottom of the vessel. The clay should be recently kneaded so that it is pliant and flexible. Take your two larger sheets and assemble them as shown in the drawing, pinching where the arrows are. Pinch all the way along the edges; they will adhere to one another. Gently shape the slabs by pushing the two joints together so that they form an opening. Now set this piece on the slab of clay that will be the bottom. Press down gently. To attach the bottom onto the body of the vessel, take some small coils of clay and place them inside the vessel around the bottom edge and, using your fingers, smooth them onto the sides and bottom to form a seal. Trim the excess clay away from the bottom slab and run your finger along the outside joint between the sides and bottom, smoothing them together. If the pot seems a little wobbly, stuff it loosely with some paper or muslin cloth and let it rest overnight before baking. The stuffing can be left in during baking.

Sheets

Vessels can also be made by draping sheets around a mold or form as opposed to slab building where the clay walls stand on their own. You can use much thinner sheets this way and layer them. Using thin sheets of the translucent clay will allow colors to show through. The mold or form is anything that can withstand the baking temperature. You could use saucers, bowls or plates from your kitchen, make a plaster mold, or make a mold from aluminum foil covered with masking tape and fabric. A simple cone made from stiff cardboard will also work. If you use glass or china and drape the clay directly onto it, the clay will be shiny where it touches the mold.

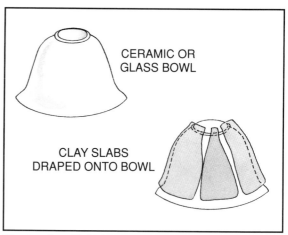

Illustration 62. Using a Form.

To avoid this effect, use some cotton sheeting or muslin to cover the mold before you drape on the clay. Look at the bowl by Grove and Grove in the photo on page 36, and Kathleen Dustin's goblets on page xii. Be sure to pinch and smooth the joins together very well. Again, it may be helpful to use the stronger clays like Promat and Fimo for the first layer. Legs can be baked separately and glued on later.

87. A bowl, paperweight and pair of earrings by **Grove and Grove**. The bowl is made of slices of geometric canes that have been layered onto a bowl form. The piece measures 7" across and is of Fimo. The paperweight is experimental and uses interesting scraps of clay with sections carved out to reveal internal patterns.

Coiling and Pinching

The next two techniques - pinch pots and coiling - are ancient methods for making vessels. Making pots in this way doesn't require anything but your hands and the clay itself, which can be very satisfying in our technological world. The pinch pot technique is used for making relatively small vessels whereas the coiling method can be used for larger pieces using thicker coils.

To make a pinch pot, start with a kneaded ball of clay about two inches in diameter and poke your thumb half way into it. Press your thumb and forefinger against the walls of the ball of clay and start pinching all the way around to make the sides. Press down to make the bottom before the sides get too thin. In general, keep the bottom and lower walls somewhat thicker for strength. Keep pinching the walls and bottom with your fingers, shaping the vessel as you go. The vessel can be gently pulled into any shape by shaping the bottom first, then stretching the walls. This is a very loose and freeform technique that is really fun to play with. Don't be too demanding with it, just experiment and let it happen. If you don't like the shape or the walls get too thin and collapse, just fold up the clay and start over again. With a little practice you will gain more and more control over the process.

To make a coil pot, start with a log of clay about one half inch thick and a foot long. Start at one end and begin to curl the clay around in a spiral to form the bottom. When the bottom is about two inches in diameter begin to coil the logs on top of one another, bringing the sides up. Press the coils together as you build the vessel. Start to smooth the bottom coils together before

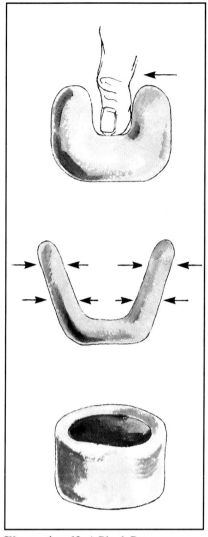

Illustration 63. A Pinch Pot.

the sides get too high. Keep adding coils and smoothing them together until the pot is as big as you want. The higher the walls, the thicker they will need to be to keep their shape. The larger the pot, the thicker the starting coils should be. If the pot gets flimsy, fill it with strips of wadded up sheeting or muslin to hold the shape. The filling can be left in while baking.

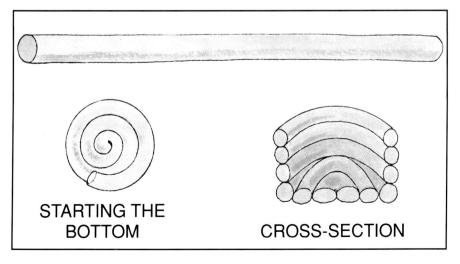

STARTING THE
BOTTOM   CROSS-SECTION

Illustration 64. A Coil Pot

88. Findings. On the left of the photo is a box by **Grove and Grove**, with a collection of findings in the top and a pair of earrings titled *Doric Columns with Angels*, by Kathleen Amt. Below is a bolo tie by **Grove and Grove**. The clock is by **City Zen Cane**. To the right is a box by **Grove and Grove** with two bracelets by **City Zen Cane**, showing the front and back surfaces. **City Zen Cane** had the elements of the bracelets made to their specifications. The boxes are made of slabs and are constructed of Fimo.

Findings & Additional Applications

Findings

The term **findings** is used by jewelers to refer to the metal or other parts necessary to attach jewelry to the human body. This includes pin backs, earring wires, posts, clips, barrettes, or straight pins. Findings may also be clock parts, mirrors, key rings, necklace clasps or even the "guts" of a kaleidoscope.

89. A close up photo of buttons on a garment by Linda Mendelson. The photo is by Charles Decker, 1987.

Necklaces

Necklace stringing is a subject in itself and I have listed several excellent books in the appendix which will be helpful. There are as many ways to fasten necklaces as there are craftspeople. The criterion for a good fastening is that it be strong, durable and attractive in appearance. Ready-made metal clasps are strong but they don't always work well in the over all design. Look at the collection of endings on page 118 for an example of many artists' solutions to this design problem. Electrical or telephone wire is a favorite solution of mine for clasps. It is brightly colored and has the same surface look as the clay. Macrame work also makes a very effective clasp. Notice the use of large end beads that go through loops and how effective they can be as a design element. The main problem with ready-made findings is that they are not an integral part of the overall piece. They can be covered and disguised or the rest of the piece can be designed around the finding. Good jewelry design will mean attention to all the details.

Fillers, spacers and other beads can be used with the polymer clay. Again, the elements that are used should be compatible with the color, shape and surface texture of the jewelry. To me, shiny metal beads are somewhat jarring in combination with dull clay beads and detract from the beauty of the intricate millefiori pattern, but this is a matter of personal preference. When designing with other beads and found objects, let these pieces guide you in your design. Use some aspect of these found pieces in the design of the clay beads to set up a dialogue between the elements. The necklace will be much more interesting in the end.

90. A collection of necklaces showing the variety of closures that may be used. Starting in the upper right and moving clockwise: a necklace by Jamey D. Allen using macrame for the closure, a necklace by Nan Roche using macrame and a loop and button for the closure, a lobster claw clasp is used in this necklace by **Grove and Grove**, another necklace by Jamey D. Allen using macrame, a necklace by Kathleen Amt using leather cord which is glued into the beads, a necklace by Pat Berlin using braided black fabric, a necklace by **City Zen Cane** with a hook and eye closure, a necklace by Kathleen Dustin making use of telephone wire and a loop and button arrangement for the clasp, and finally a metal box clasp is used in this necklace by Pier Voulkos. Notice the use of the signature in the pieces by Pier Voulkos and Pat Berlin.

Pins and Earrings

A large variety of ready made findings can be purchased for pins and earrings. Pins backs are readily available and cheap but not especially attractive. The metal back can be embedded in the clay before baking to hide it or it can be covered with enamel or a piece of suede after baking and gluing, giving you great flexibility in pin design. Pin backs and ear wires may also be easily made with silver wire and jeweler's pliers. When making ear wires make sure to put a few kinks in the embedded end to prevent it from pulling out of the clay after baking. You can make your own pins by filing one end of the wire into a sharp point and making a loop in the other end as a closure. Check out the suppliers listing in the appendix for sources of ready-made findings and jewelry supplies.

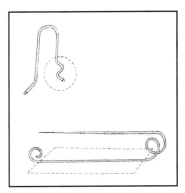

Illustration 65. Findings.

91. A selection of books by Kathleen Amt. In the back is a photo album bound by the artist with a polymer clay inlay. To the right are three bound journals, *Kimono Journal*, *Night Journal*, and *Flower Journal* with polymer clay beads worked into the bindings and clay catches. On the left is a book titled *Temple Book*, which is entirely of polymer clay. Below is a book titled *Fish Tales*. The covers are of polymer clay and the interior is marbled papers of fishes that are structured as an accordion. To the right is the book *Water Babies* made entirely of polymer clay. Notice the artist's use of the printing inlay technique which she developed. Finally is a small book titled *Mermaid and Bird*. When opened, a paper accordion unfolds. The largest book is 18" and the smallest is 2.5".

Other Applications

There are many other applications that are wonderfully suited to the use of polymer clay. I will briefly touch on some of these ideas but your mind and imagination will fill in the spaces.

Books

The work of Kathy Amt is a marvelous example of the extension of ideas and techniques from the disciplines of the book arts to the use of polymer clay. She has used the

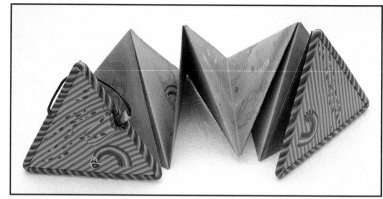

92. A triangular book, titled *Only the Rain Can Make the Colors Glow* by Kathleen Amt. The covers are of polymer clay (Sculpey III) and the dimensions are 3" x 3" x 3". Notice the artists use of candy cane to edge the covers and the clever catch.

clay in every possible way in her books. The clay has been used as an inset in a book cover, as elements in the bindings, and as the pages themselves. She uses collage and paper, printing techniques, and pop-up book concepts in combination within her books. A fascination with games and toys is also apparent in much of her work. Look at the Jacob's ladder of strongmen on page 84 and the Mermaid book on page 81 (photo 54).

Bracelets

The collection of bracelets made by Petronella Daubin are remarkable for their strength and flexibility. They were made of Fimo and baked for an extra long time. Some of them have a metal wire running through them but the broad flat bracelets are clay only. Many other designs for bracelets come to mind. Hinged or linked bracelets, strings of beads, or flat designs are all possible. Pay attention to costume jewelry at the store and antique museum pieces for inspiration.

93. A collection of bracelets by **Petronella Daubin**. The thinner bracelets have a wire armature running through them forming the catch, and are very flexible. The thicker bracelets have some flex but are made of solid Fimo.

Buttons

Buttons are a perfect use for the clay. How many times have you looked for just the right color and size button and couldn't find it? Knitters, seamstresses and weavers will love this clay.

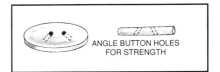

Illustration 66. Buttons.

The buttons can be made in any size and shape and, best of all, the color can be perfectly matched. The clay is fully washable and can be drycleaned. Fimo, Cernit or Promat would be the brands of choice because of their strength.

Buttons can be made by using an old button and covering it with a sheet of clay. Surface canes may be applied. A metal button blank designed to be covered with fabric also works well. Buttons do not need to have an underlying blank if they are thick enough to withstand handling. Remember that buttons need to withstand a lot of strain. Buttons can be made as a flat plate with two or four pierced holes. Another design has a small loop of wire as a sewing spot, or a slightly raised back that is pierced may also work. The clay must be thick enough for strength, and the button must be engineered properly for attachment. A method of piercing that will help reinforce a button with holes is shown in the illustration. If the holes are pierced at an angle, the top aspect of the button will look ordinary but the volume of clay between the holes will be increased and add strength. Its a matter of engineering. Look through your grandmother's button jar for inspiration.

Button design should not be haphazard. It can make or break a garment. Buttons should be an integral part of the design of the whole garment, using color or shape to play off of elements in the garment. Refer back to the color and design chapter for ideas about design. Linda Mendelsons' wonderful knitted garments are enhanced by her use of buttons to pick up color and shape themes from the fabric.

94. This knitted coat is by Linda Mendelson. Notice the artist's use of the polymer clay buttons as an integral design element of the piece. The photo is by Charles Decker, 1987.

Wall Pieces

Wall pieces are another great application for the clay. It is light weight and can be used with any or all of the techniques covered. One idea might be to take an impressions of brass plaques or stone carvings. These pieces could be used together with other collage objects. Don't forget about patchwork as a source of inspiration.

95. A wall piece by Lois Brant, titled *Pearly Nights*. The artist has used pearlescent powders on the fabric-like elements of the design.

96. A wall piece titled *Black & White Pointed Star* by Abby Rohrer. Piece measures about 5" x 8".

Bolo Ties, Hair Clips, and Buckles

Bolo ties, hair clips and belt buckles are other applications of the clay for ornamentation. You will have to experiment with these items as there are so many different ways to design them. You need to consider the kind of conditions the piece will be likely to experience. Belt buckles, for instance, take a lot of punishment. Be sure to give the finished pieces a good road test before selling them.

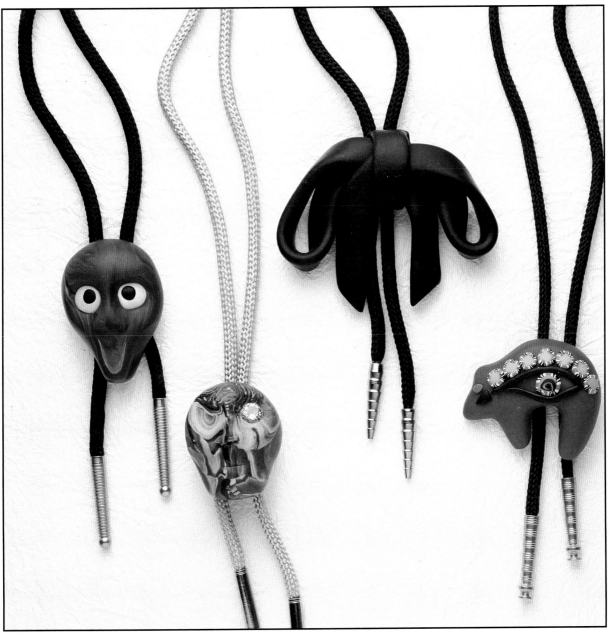

97. A collection of bolo ties by David Edwards. From left to right: *Goggle-Eyed Mask*, *Mask with Zirconia Eye*, *Floppy Bow Tie*, and *Bear Fetish*. The artist works in Fimo. The bow tie measures 3.5" in length.

Clocks and Mirrors

Clocks and mirrors may be covered with clay and baked. Old tin boxes or even cigar boxes may be covered with sheets of clay and baked. Remember, any thing that can withstand the baking temperatures will work quite well.

98. A pendulum clock and two frames by Martha Breen of **Urban Tribe**.

Afterword

The ideas and techniques described in this book are only a starting place from which to develop your own. As you start to work with these wonderful clays, you will surely make many more discoveries to add to your repertoire of techniques. The material seems to pull you into experimentation and creativity. I hope you will be able to return to the book again and again for inspiration and fresh approaches to your own work, whether in polymer clay or other media.

99. A small kaleidoscope necklace and matching pin by Steve and Carmen Colley of **Gallo-Colley Glass**. The kaleidosculpture is titled *Solaris* and measures 3" in length.

Imitation is a fine way to learn. Even the Old Masters copied each others paintings to learn techniques, Picasso's cubism was inspired by African artists. We all are influenced by what we see, consciously or unconsciously, but, stay true to your own vision.

The 40 artists whose work appear in this book have generously shared their images and techniques with you. Please respect their work. Let their work inspire your own creations, but do not copy their work as your own. Let every piece you make be your own creation.

Have fun! But, be very careful, this stuff is highly addictive. The author also disavows any responsibility for lost sleep and irate family members due to late nights working with this wonderful new clay!

100. *The Destroyer* by Wilcke Smith.

About Plastics & Hazards

Let me put in a good word about understanding your material. Although as an artist and craftsperson you are primarily concerned with design and inspiration, your work should also be durable and well crafted. A beautiful design means nothing if it falls apart in the wearer's hands. A thorough understanding of your working materials is essential for you to be able to have full command of your artistic process. I think this is especially true for plastics as they are relative newcomers to the art world and there is less accurate, popularized knowledge floating about.

Polyvinyl chloride has been produced commercially since the 1930's in Germany. During and after the Second World War, it began to be manufactured extensively as an inexpensive rubber substitute. This was made possible by the development of plasticizers and other additives which produced very flexible forms of PVC.

Polyvinyl chlorides (PVC's) are some of the most heavily used plastics in our world today. Phonograph records, garden hoses, shoe soles, automotive parts and toys are just some of the items present in our daily lives. One of the reasons for this heavy usage is that PVC can be compounded into many different forms: rigid, rubbery, transparent, opaque, brittle, or soft and moldable. This is achieved by mixing various additives into the basic material before heating to harden it.

First, lets start with a few definitions. Polymer means many units of a molecule, in this case vinyl chloride, strung together. Polyvinyl chloride is a polymer and polymerization is the chemical process of making a polymer. There are five basic steps involved in producing the hardened final product. The first three of these, synthesis, polymerization, and compounding, generate the polymer clay that we get in packages from the art store. I will give you a brief overview of these processes. The final two, forming and fusing are what you will be doing after you bring the clay home. The latter are the subject of this book.

Synthesis, the first step in the production of polyvinyl chloride, is the process of making the vinyl chloride monomer or single unit that gets strung together to produce polyvinyl chloride. The monomer looks like this in chemical notation:

-CH$_2$CHCl-

It consists of 2 carbon atoms, 3 hydrogen atoms and a chloride atom arranged in a chain. The vinyl chloride monomer (VCM) can be synthesized in many ways but two methods predominate. The oldest method is to react inexpensive hydrochloric acid and acetylene together which yields

VCM and water as products. A newer and more economically efficient method of synthesis is to react ethylene gas and chlorine, a process called oxychlorination. Most monomer today is made by this second method. The VCM produced is a gas at room temperature and is stored under pressure as a liquid, ready for the next step.

The next step is to string together all the monomers into a chain. This is called polymerization and converts vinyl chloride monomer (VCM) gas into polyvinyl chloride (PVC) particles like grains of sand. There are several different methods currently used for this step. The type of polymerization used, causes variations in the PVC particles produced, particularly in grain size. Manufacturers will buy different kinds of PVC raw powders depending on the type of products and methods of manufacture that they will be using. Our polymer clay uses a powder with a very fine grain size.

The three primary polymerization process are called the emulsion process, the suspension or solution process and the bulk or mass process, in order of development. The suspension process is by far the most widely used method, accounting for 80% of all PVC, but it is the emulsion method which is used for the production of PVC that is the raw material for plastisols, the group of plastics to which polymer clay belongs. The VCM gas is pumped into the reaction vessel with catalysts, chemicals which assist the reaction, and put under pressure. The VCM molecules then link up with one another, forming chains of polyvinyl chloride. These chains will curl up into microscopic grains. When the reaction is complete, the reaction vessel is depressurized and the PVC is removed from the walls and dried, yielding PVC powder. With all of these methods, there is a certain amount of residual VCM left after the reaction which must be reclaimed because of the health hazards involved.

After polymerization, various chemicals are added to the polymer grains to enhance its molding and melting characteristics. This is called compounding. Colorants are added as well as inert fillers like calcium carbonate, clay or silica gel. An antioxidant is added to resist discoloration and as a heat stabilizer. The bulk of the additives are plasticizers, which increase the softness and malleability of the PVC and assist in the fusion and melt at low temperatures. Indeed, without plasticizers, the PVC polymer would be too brittle and unstable to be usable. The discovery of plasticizers in Germany in the 1930's was crucial to the evolution of PVC usage in our modern world. The whole chemistry might have been abandoned were it not for their discovery. The role of plasticizers in the eventual end product is complex and even today is not fully understood. The type of plasticizer, the amount added, and the temperature at which it is mixed with the polymer grains, can produce anything from a clear, rigid plastic to a soft, moldable, opaque plastic like polymer clay, and a whole range of types in between. One of the most commonly used plasticizers, is an organic compound called dioctyl phthalate or DOP. The correct proportion of DOP mixed with the polymer will produce a plastisol. Any more or any less will produce plastics which are not malleable. The oily looking ring left on a sheet of paper by uncooked polymer clay is most likely left by the DOP leaching out. There are many other possible compounds that can be added to PVC, but many of these are specific to industrial applications where special problems may arise, like sticking to molding equipment, and may not be used in polymer clay.

The manufacturers of Sculpey, Fimo and Cernit probably use different types of plasticizers from brand to brand and even within their own product lines. This may account for the differences in malleability between Sculpey III and Promat, and Fimo colors and Fimo transparent.

Forming and gelation are the final two steps. These are the ones we are most concerned with understanding. This book covers the enormous range of possible forming techniques, so I will describe gelation in more detail here.

The final step, called gelation, is the mysterious process by which soft, moldable polymer clay is transformed into a hard permanent plastic by heat. It is also called melting or fusion in the industry and much has been written about what is actually happening in this process. It is conceptually similar to what would happen if you melted loose pellets of wax together in a pan without allowing them to melt completely into a liquid. They would slowly fuse into a solid mass that would conform to the shape of the pan. In PVC fusion, the polymer molecules are arranged into grains which are porous. They are saturated with the plasticizer which keeps them in a malleable suspension. As the grains are gradually heated, they swell into a gel and begin to fuse with each other. As the temperature rises further, the fused PVC forms a hard permanent plastic. Optimum fusion temperatures vary slightly between the different polymer clays due to the differences in additives used; between 250°F - 300°F are the stated temperatures to achieve full fusion.[9]

HAZARDS

Generally, the two ingredients which might present some hazard with very heavy usage are residual vinyl chloride monomer and the plasticizers, like dioctyl phthalate, that make the clay malleable.

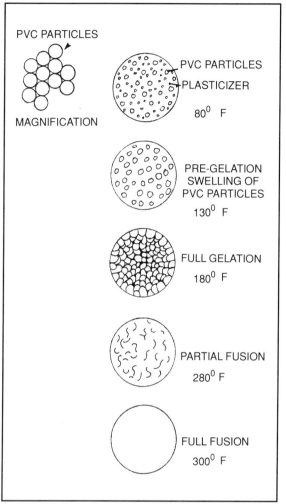

Illustration 67. Polyvinyl Chloride Fusion.

As for vinyl chloride monomer, any residual VCM is carefully removed from the polymer long before compounding into the clay. The dioctyl phthalate is an organic, petroleum product and is listed as a hazardous chemical by OSHA. It is present in about 15% concentration in the polymer clay and leaches out from the unbaked clay. As long as polymer clay is in its original plastic wrapper, you need not worry about what it comes into contact with. You may notice when you remove the wrapper and place the clay on a piece of paper, an oily ring is left after a few hours. This ring is caused by plasticizer leaching out. The plasticizer is considered hazardous, so polymer clay should not be used within the vicinity of food or food-using utensils or surfaces. Once polymer clay has been cooked and hardened it becomes essentially inert and should be considered non-toxic for ordinary use.

I would add a word of caution, however, about making objects out of polymer clay that might be used for food containers. PVC, and almost all plastics, are porous and may have some amount of residual plasticizer left, even after hardening, that could be released by acidic foods or liquids. For this reason, do not use tools or surfaces which might come in contact with foods, wash your hands carefully after working with it, and do not use PVC containers to store food products.

Selected Bibliography

Color and Design

Itten, Johannes. **The Elements of Color.** Translated by Ernst Van Hagen. Van Nostrand Reinhold, New York. 1970. ISBN 0-442-24038-4. Still the best book on color.

Mills, Jane and Janet K. Smith. **Design Concepts.** Fairchild Publications, Division of Capital Cities Media, Inc. New York. 1985. A simple and straightforward workbook on design.

Proctor, Richard M. **The Principals of Pattern for Craftsmen and Designers.** Van Nostrand Reinhold, New York. 1969. ISBN 0-442-26639-1. An excellent source of inspiration for pattern formation.

Stockton, James. **Designer's Guide to Color.** Chronicle Books. 1984. ISBN 0-87701-317-9. See also volumes 2, 3, 4 and 5. These books are simply color swatches and combinations that may be helpful to suggest color usage with polymer clay.

Wong, Wucius. **Principles of Color Design.** Van Nostrand Reinhold, New York. 1986. ISBN 0-442-29284-8.

Wong, Wucius. **Principles of Two-Dimensional Design.** Van Nostrand Reinhold, New York. 1972.

Beads and Glassworking

Dubin, Lois Sherr. **The History of Beads from 30,000 B.C. to the Present.** Harry N. Abrams, Inc. Publishers, New York. 1987. ISBN 0-8109-0736-4. An outstanding and inspirational book.

Allen, Jamey D. "Cane Manufacture for Mosaic Glass Beads: Part I," *Ornament* 5(4):6-11, 1982; and "Part II," *Ornament* 6(1):13,43, 1983. Explains cane manufacture in glass.

Allen, Jamey D. "Chevron Star Rosetta Beads: Part I," *Ornament* 7(1):19-24, 40; "Part II," 7(2):24-29,40;

"Part III," 7(3):24-27,41; "Part IV," 7(4):24-26, 42-47.

DeCarlo, Giacomo. "Jacopo Franchini: Miniature Portraits in Glass," *Ornament* 10(4): 46-47, 1987.

Francis, Peter. "Bead Report XX: Another Bead Potpourri," *Ornament* 10(3):62- 63, 75-79, 1987.

Goldstein, Sidney M. **Pre-Roman and Early Roman Glass in the Corning Museum of Glass.** Dover Publishing, Mineola, NY. 1979.

Grose, David Frederick. **Early Ancient Glass.** Hudson Hills Press, New York, 1989.

Liu, R.K. "Faience: Technical Aspects and Beads of Simple Form", *The Bead Journal*, Vol. 1(4):24-41, 1975.

Picard, John and Ruth Picard. **Beads from the West African Trade. Vol. 1: Chevrons, Vol. II: Tabular Beads, Vol. III: Fancy Beads, Vol. IV: White Hearts, Feather Eye Beads, and Vol. V: Russian Beads and Vol VI: Millefiori Beads from the West African Trade.** Published by Picard African Imports, 9310 Los Prados, Carmel, CA, 93923. These pamphlets are beautifully photographed collections of Venetian beads and are very inspiring for imitation with polymer clay.

Stout, Ann M. "The Archaeological Context of Late Roman Period Mosaic Glass Face Beads", *Ornament*, Vol. 9(4):58-61, 76-77, 1986.

Ukai, Nancy. "Kyoyo Asao, Tombodama/Glass Bead Master", *Ornament*, Vol. 4(3):13-18, 1980. A modern glass beadmaker who uses caneworking techniques.

Ukai, Nancy. "Kyoyo Asao: Glass Bead Master, New Work", *Ornament*, Vol. 7(3):2-5, 1984.

Polymer Clay References

Allen, Jamey D. "Millifiori Polyform Techniques," *Ornament* Vol.12(4):46-49, Summer 1989.

Carlson, Maureen. **Jewelry: Create One-of-a-Kind Jewelry with Oven Baked Modeling Compounds.** Vol. 3. videotape. 1990. Write to: "Wee Folk Creations," 18476 Natchez Ave., Prior Lake, MN 55372. Telephone: 612 447-3828.

Cohn, Tony. **Jewelry, Magnets and More: Techniques, Tools and Temperatures for Using Cernit #1.** Published by Handcraft Designs, 63 E. Broad Street, Hatfield, PA 19440. 1989. Telephone: 215 855-3022.

Dustin, Kathleen. "The Use of Polyform in Bead-Making," *Ornament* Vol. 11(3):16-19, Spring 1988.

Dustin, Kathleen. "No Limits For Polymer Clay," *Craft*, October 1988.

Edwards, David. **Using Fimo: A Basic Handbook.** Published by David Edwards. 1990. Write to: David Edwards, Mail Code H-756, UCSD, 225 Dickinson St., San Diego, CA 92103.

Hamaker, Barbara. "Tory Hughes Jewelry, Art Is a Conversation Not a Conversation Piece," *Ornament* 13(2): 60-63,6, 1989.

Jensen, Gay, "Discover Polymer Clay," *Shuttle, Spindle & Dyepot.* Vol. 22 (1): 46-49, Winter 1990/91.

Roche, Nan, "Creating with Polymers," *Shuttle Spindle & Dyepot.* Vol 22 (1): 52-53, Winter 1990/91.

Searle, Karen, "Savage Adornments for the Civilized: William Farra." *Ornament.* Vol. 13 (4): 60-63, Summer 1990.

Whitaker, Joyce and Jamey D. Allen. "Discovering Some of Polyforms Possibilities...", Beadesigner International Newsletter, Fall/Winter 1989. 132 Antrim St. Cambridge, MA 02139.

Whitaker, Joyce, Lori Schill and Stephanie Betlyon. "Polyform Possibilities, Part II", "Some Fimo Information", "More on Conditioning Fimo", Beadesigner International Newsletter, Spring/Summer 1989.

Whitaker, Joyce, and Jamey D. Allen ed. "The Polyform Papers", a booklet available from Beadesigner International, 132 Antrim St. #2, Cambridge, MA 02139.

Fiber Related References

Andersen, Lee. You Knit Unique, Inspiration and Information for the Original Knitter. Vibrant Publishing, 9 Kent Terrace, Wellington, New Zealand. 1985. The book contains a section on embellishments including the use of Fimo for buttons. It also has a wonderful color and design chapter for fiber artists.

Andersen, Lee. **You and Yours. Extra Ordinarily You. Reflections of You.** With polymer clay graphics by Kathy Amt. Vibrant Publishing, 9 Kent Terrace, Wellington, New Zealand. 1990. In Press. These three volumes are wonderfully illustrated knitting books where the border graphics are made of polymer clay by Kathy Amt. This is a totally novel use of the material.

Bradkin, Cheryl Greider. **The Seminole Patchwork Book.** Yours Truly, Inc. 5455 Garden Grove Boulevard, Westminster, CA 92683. ISBN 0-932946-03-8, 1980. A great source of inspiration for Seminole patchwork patterns that may be translated into polymer clay.

Dale, Julie Schafler. **Art to Wear.** Abbeville Press, New York, 1988. ISBN 0- 89659-664-8.

Schiff, Stefan O. **Buttons: Art in Miniature.** Lancaster-Miller Inc., Berkeley, CA. 1979. ISBN 0-89581-013-1.

Metalworking

Untracht, Oppi. **Jewelry Concepts and Technology.** Doubleday and Co., Inc., Garden City, New York, 1982. ISBN 0-385-04185-3. The technique called "mokume gane" is discussed in detail along with many other metalworking techniques.

Untracht, Oppi. **Metal Techniques for Craftsman.** Doubleday and Co., Garden City, NY. 1975. ISBN 0-385-03027-4

McCallum, Alistair. "The Technique of Mokume Gane", *Crafts*, No.42 Jan/Feb 1980. pp. 20-21.

Ceramic Related References

Coyne, John. "Night Garden with Ladies: Jane Peiser," Penland School of Crafts Book of Pottery, pp. 58-74. Bobbs-Merrill, New York. 1975.

Kajitani, Ban. "Neriage and Nerikomi Techniques," *Ceramics Monthly* 27(2):50-55, 1979. This article discusses layering techniques that can be translated with polymer clay.

Finishing Techniques for Jewelry

Champion, Dave. **The Basics of Bead Stringing.** Bourget, Santa Monica, CA. 1985. ISBN 0-9615353-0-X.

Coles, Janet and Robert Budwig. **The Book of Beads - A Practical and Inspirational Guide to Beads and Jewelry Making.** Simon and Schuster. 1990.

Poris, Ruth F. **Advanced Beadwork**. Golden Hands Press, Farmington Hills, MI. 1990.

Poris, Ruth F. **Step by Step Bead Stringing.** Golden Hands Press, Farmington Hills, MI. 1984.

Tomalin, Stefany. **Beads: Make Your Own Unique Jewelry.** David and Charles, England. Distributed by Sterling Publishing Co., New York, NY. 1988. ISBN 0- 7153-9105-4.

Plastics

Davidov, Corinne and Ginny Redington Dawes. **The Bakelite Jewelry Book.** Abbeville Press, New York, NY, 1988. ISBN 0-89659-867-5.

Katz, Sylvia. **Early Plastics.** Shire Album # 168. Shire Publications, Ltd. 1986. ISBN 0-85263-790-X.

Katz, Sylvia. **Plastics: Common Objects, Classic Designs.** Thames and Hudson, Ltd. London, 1984. ISBN 0-8109-0769-0.

Burgess, R.H. ed., **Manufacturing and Processing of PVC.** Macmillan Publishing Co, Inc., New York. 1982.

Sarvetnick, Harold. **Polyvinyl Chloride.** Van Nostrand Reinhold. 1969.

Project Books

Romantic Brooches Made of Fimo, Adolf Thiemann GmbH, P.O.B. 1046, 4440 Rheine, West Germany. ISBN 3-921891-09-4. Marlis Meyer. #8712 01 GB.

Fimo: Ideas for Creative Modelling, Eberhard Faber GmbH, D-8430 Neumarkt, West Germany, 1988. #8717 GB.

Modelling Fashionable Jewelry with Fimo, Eberhard Faber GmbH., D-8430 Neumarkt, West Germany, 1987. Evelyn Gessert-Tschakert. #8720 02 GB.

New Fimo Modelling Ideas, Eberhard Faber GmbH., D-8430 Neumarkt, West Germany, 1986. #8720 01 GB.

Modelling with Fimo, Adolf Thiemann GmbH & Co. Postfach 1046, 4440 Rheine, West Germany, 1984. Ursula Hollmann. #8713 GB.

Dollmaking Books

Carlson, Maureen. **Mug Dwellers and Wee Folk,** Vol. 1., 1989 and Vol. 2. **Faces, Faces, Faces.** 1990 In videotape. Write to: Wee Folk Creations, 18476 Natchez Ave., Prior Lake, MN 55372. Telephone: 612 447-3828.

Ericson, Rolf. **Sculpting Little People.** Vols. 1 & 2. 1983. Published by Seeley's Ceramic Service, Inc., 9 River Street, Oneonta, NY 13820. Telephone: 607 432- 3812.

Goldstein, Louis. **Doll Sculpting, Start to Finish.** Scott Advertising and Publishing Co., 30595 W. 8 Mile Rd., Livonia, MI 48152. 1985, 1987. ISBN 0-916809-17-X.

Lucchesi, Bruno and Margit Malmstrom. **Modeling the Figure in Clay, A Sculptor's Guide to Anatomy**. Watson-Guptill Publications, New York, 1980 ISBN 0-8230-3097-0.

Olson, Ester. **Fimo Sweets,** Boynton & Associates, Inc., Clifton, VA. 1983. ISBN 0-933168-28-4.

Oroyan, Susanna and Carol Rossel Waugh. **Contemporary Artists' Dolls.** Hobby House Press, Cumberland, MD. 1985. ISBN 0-87588-271-4.

Oroyan, Susanna. **The Dollmaker's Notebook, Working with Sculpey.** 1983. Write to: Susanna Oroyan, 1880 Parliament St., Eugene, OR 97405.

Rutenberg, Irena. **The Body in Motion.** Vol. 1. **Heads: Woman, Man and Child. Vol 2.** Hands and Feet: Arms and Legs. **Vol 3.** In preparation (Jan. 1991) to be published by Mimi's Books and Supplies for the Serious Dollmaker, P.O. Box 662, Point Pleasant, NJ 08742. Telephone: 201 889-0804.

GLOSSARY

Achromatic - Free from color.

Amaté - A type of Mexican bark cloth paper made by pounding softened bark into sheets.

Analogous Colors - A group of hues that lie side-by-side on the color wheel.

Armature - A skeletal framework built as a support on which a clay, wax, or plaster figure is constructed. It supports the sculpture and reduces the amount of clay needed.

Bas-relief - A relief sculpture in which figures project slightly from the background.

Cane - A term borrowed from glassworking referring to glass rods either plain or with a pattern running through them, to be used as an addition to glass pieces. Canes were used to make millefiori beads.

Clay - A very fine suspension of aluminum silicate that is moldable when wet and can be fused by very high temperatures into a permanent form.

Chasing - To ornament metal by engraving.

Chroma - The purity of a color or its freedom from white or gray.

Chromatic - Pertaining to color or colors.

Faience - An artificial compound made of quartz grains in a doughy suspension which is partially fused by heat. It is often self-glazing and can be cast into molds. It is possibly an ancestor of glass.

Glass - A hard, brittle, noncrystalline transparent substance produced by fusion at high temperatures, of silicates containing soda and lime.

Hue - The color of an object, classified as red, blue, green or yellow in reference to the spectrum.

Inlay - The insetting of a piece of clay into a space in another piece of clay.

Intaglio - Refers to recessed carving as opposed to carving in relief.

Kaolin - A very fine white clay used in the manufacture of porcelain.

Lamination - A construct often of wood, made of layer upon layer.

Loaf - A block of clay having a complex pattern running throughout, usually square or rectangular in shape.

Log - A thicker roll of clay used interchangeably with the word cane.

Marquetry - A woodworking technique that involves inlaying colored woods into a background.

Millefiori - An Italian glassworking term, meaning 'thousand flowers' that Venetian glassworkers used to describe their copies of ancient mosaic glass. It refers to decorative glass rods or canes made by fusing multicolored elements together, cutting them crosswise, and melting them onto the surface of beads or other objects.

Mokume Gane - A Japanese term borrowed from metalsmithing. It means "wood grain metal" and refers to the growth rings in trees. Various colors of metals are laminated together, positive and negative spaces are cut out of the laminate and it is rolled through a rolling mill creating a pattern similar to annular growth rings in wood.

Monochromatic - Colors made from tints and shades of the same hue.

Monomer - A small molecule that is capable of reacting with other small molecules to produce a polymer.

Mosaic Glass - Any vessel or object made of fused segments of polychrome glass canes.

Onlay - The application of a piece of clay onto the surface of another piece of clay.

Oxychlorination - The name of the reaction most commonly used to make vinyl chloride monomer.

Organic - As it pertains to chemistry, this term refers to compounds that are derived from plants or animals. Petroleum is the liquid remains of ancient forests and consists of complex mixtures of hydrocarbons.

Repoussé - A term borrowed from metalworking where hammer and punches are used on sheet metal to push a design through from the back.

Plastic - A generic term, referring to any group of synthetic or natural materials which may be shaped when soft and then hardened, including many types of resins (amber), resinoids, polymers, cellulose derivatives, casein materials, and proteins.

Plasticizer - Any of a group of organic substances which are used in plastics to impart viscosity, flexibility, softness or other properties to the finished product.

Plastisol - A soft, flexible compound resulting from the mixture of plastic polymer with plasticizer.

Polymer - A compound of high molecular weight derived by the chemical linking together of many small molecules into a chain.

Polyvinyl Chloride - A white, water insoluble, thermoplastic resin (-CH2CHCl-)n derived by the polymerization of vinyl chloride; used chiefly as a coating for phonographic records, in the manufacture of floor coverings and as an insulator for metal pipes and wire.

Saturation - The degree of chroma or purity of a color; the degree or freedom from admixture with white.

Shade - The degree of darkness of a color determined by the quantity of black added.

Snake - For polymer clay working, this term refers to a small log usually of a single color.

Stamping - A patterned tool is impressed or forcibly struck into a piece of metal or clay.

Tint - A color diluted with white.

Value - The degree of lightness or darkness in a color.

Artist Listing.

At the end of each listing are the plate numbers indicating where the artist's work may be seen.

Jamey D. Allen
P.O. Box 14724
San Francisco, CA 94114
707 584-3568
Plate #'s: 19, 24, 25, 26, 51, 58, 90

Kathleen Amt
Torpedo Factory Art Center #14
105 North Union St.
Alexandria, VA 22314
703 836-5807 or 301 864-0602
Plate #'s: 4, 28, 53, 54, 56, 57, 58, 63, 88, 90, 91, 92

Helen Banes
The Fiber Gallery
The Torpedo Factory Art Center
105 North Union St.
Alexandria, VA 22314
703 836-5807
Plate #: 67

Deborah Banyas & T.P. Speer
181 Forest St.
Oberlin, OH 44074
216 774-8319
Plate #'s: 26, 80

Pat Berlin
928 Mackall Ave.
McLean, VA 22101
703 356-4954
Plate #'s: 17, 90

Lois N. Brant
7728 Viceroy St.
Springfield, VA 22151
703 569-4963
Plate #: 95

Martha Breen
Urban Tribe
415 540-5837
Plate #'s: 15, 19, 98

Maureen Carlson
Wee Folk Creations
18476 Natchez Ave.
Prior Lake, MN 55372
612 447-3828
Plate #'s: 75, 79

Stephen and Carmen Colley
519 Artemis Dr.
San Antonio, TX 78218
512 654-3344
Plate #: 99

Kathleen Dustin
Torpedo Factory Art Center #25
105 North Union St.
Alexandria, VA 22314
Plate #'s: 2, 17, 19, 26, 49, 51, 55, 57, 86, 90

David Edwards
Mail Code H-756, U.C.S.D.
225 Dickinson Street
San Diego, CA 92103
619 543-3932
Plate #: 97

Janice Farley
175 Franklin St.
New York, NY 10013
212 431-6162
Plate #: 84

Wayne Farra
Studio One of a Kind
518 E. Wilson St. #1
Madison, WI 53703
608 255-6261
Plate #: 69

Steven Ford & David Forlano
City Zen Cane
1714 N. Mascher At. 3rd Floor
Philadelphia, PA 19122
215 739-0609
Plate #'s: 4, 14, 28, 39, 88, 90

Cathy Glasson
Art Necko
229 Grand St.
New York, NY 10013
212 431-3313
Plate #: 35

Michael & Ruth Ann Grove
1509 San Pablo Ave.
Berkeley, CA 94702
415 524-5549
Plate #'s: 4, 19, 28, 37, 57, 59, 87, 88, 90

Karen Hubert
The Torpedo Factory Art Center
105 N. Union St. #3
Alexandria, VA 22314
703 683-3004
Plate #: 11

Tory Hughes
125 West Richmond St.
Pt. Richmond, CA 94801
415 236-0532
Plate #'s: 7, 71, 74

Alliah Kahn & Ann L.Kahn & Lois
    Grommesh
    Their work can be found at the
    Portland Saturday Market or:
    8700 S. W. 26th St
    Portland, OR 97219
    503 245-6866
    Plate #'s: 6, 10

Doug Kennedy
    1240 Hayes St. #3
    San Francisco, CA 94117
    415 474-4828
    Plate #'s: 78, 81

Jane van der Kuil
    15816 Wolf Meadows Drive
    Grass Valley, CA 95949
    Plate #'s: 73, 82

Patricia Kutza
    P.O. Box 904
    El Cerrito, CA 94530
    415 522-6137
    Plate #: 62

Jeffrey Kyle
    The Big Bang
    616 S.W. Park Ave.
    Portland, OR 97205
    503 274-1741
    Plate #: 76

Claire Laties
    119 Betsy Williams Dr.
    Edgewood, RI 02905
    Plate #: 61

Joe Lee
    800 West That Rd.
    Bloomington, IN 47403
    812 824-8291
    Plate #: 70

Mary Huart Mazer
    P.O. Box 344
    Glen Echo, MD 20812
    301 564-3738
    Plate #'s: 80, 101

Linda Mendelson
    Julie Artisans Gallery
    687 Madison Ave.
    New York, NY 10021
    212 688-2345
    Plate #'s: 20, 89, 94

Lee Meyers
    Plate #: 17

Lindly Haunani Miller
    4826 N. 25th St.
    Arlington, VA 22207
    703 243-6841
    Plate #'s: 32, 40

Elke Kuhn Moore
    137 Atlantic Ave.
    Brooklyn, NY 11201
    718 875-6357
    Plate #: 43

Perry, Katrina
    Plate #: 19

Petronella Daubin
    Plate #: 93

Diane Plumley
    30-11 34th St. #5E
    Astoria, NY 11103
    718 545-4624
    Plate #: 77

Nan Roche
    4511 Amherst Rd.
    College Park, MD 20740
    301 864-1805
    Plate #'s: 9, 19, 26, 45, 47, 52, 90

Abby Rohrer
    c/o Judy Braune
    8216 Hillcrest Rd.
    Annandale, VA 22003
    703 280-2721
    Plate #'s 8, 96

Marie Segal Artist/Designer
    The Clay Factory
    525 N. Andreasen Suite G
    Escondido, CA 92025
    619 741-3242 or
    1-800-243-3466
    Plate #'s: 58, 85

Sarah Shriver
    8 Redding Way
    San Rafael, CA 94901
    Plate #: 36

Wilcke Smith
    3616 Dakota N.E.
    Albuquerque, NM 87110
    505 881-8321
    Plate #: 72, 100

Spirit Scopes
    P.O. Box 747
    Saluda, NC 28773
    Plate #: 83

Ingrid Frances Stark
    Dragonlady Designs
    520 Christianson Ave.
    Madison, WI 53714
    608 246-4312
    Plate #: 68

Jeanne Sturdevant
    P.O. Box 1021
    Greenville, TX 75403-1021
    214 454-7234
    Plate #: 31

Lynne Sward
    625 Bishop Dr.
    Virginia Beach, VA 23455
    804 497-7917
    Plate #'s: 16, 19, 28

Jo-Ellen Trilling
    43 E. 60th St. A-62
    New York, NY 10022
    212 980-1359
    Plate #: 70

Pier Voulkos
    105 Clinton St. #8
    New York, NY 10002
    212 420-8434
    Plate #'s: 19, 21, 22, 38, 50, 90

Ellen Watt
    Wear Art
    365 Orms St.
    Providence, RI 02908
    401 274-5192
    Plate #: 34

Kaz Yamashita
    603 S. Carolina Ave. S.E.
    Washington, DC 20003
    202 544-4620
    Plate #'s: 9, 30, 64

Suppliers

CLAYS

Wholesalers

1. American Art Clay Co., Inc.
   4717 W. Sixteenth St.
   Indianapolis, IN 4622-2598
   (317) 244-6871 or (800) 428-3239
   FAX: (317) 240-4208

The American Art Clay Company, Inc. is a major importer and distributor of FIMO and other craft materials.

2. The Clay Factory
   Howard & Marie Segal
   P.O. Box 1270
   Escondido, CA 92025
   619 741-3242 or
   800 783-3466

The Clay Factory is one of many distributors of Fimo made by Eberhard Faber in Germany. They carry the whole line of Eberhard Faber tools, books, powders etc. They are a great resource for all kinds of information about polymer clays. They also now carry Cernit.

3. Dee's Delights, Inc.
   3150 Stateline Rd.
   Cincinnati, OH 45052
   513 353-3390

Importer, leading wholesale minature and dollhouse distributors. They carry Fimo.

4. Handcraft Designs, Inc.
   Tony Kohn
   63 East Broad St.
   Hatfield, PA 19440
   215 855-3022

They are the major importers of Cernit brand polymer clay from Germany. Cernit comes in 37 colors. They also have published a project book entitled, "Jewelry, Magnets and More: Techniques, Tools and Temperatures for using Cernit # 1," for $4.95.

5. Polyform Products, Inc.
   9420 Byron St.
   P.O. Box 2119
   Schiller Park, IL 60176
   708 678-4836

The only American manufacturer of polymer clay, it makes Sculpey, Super Sculpey, Sculpey III (which comes in 30 colors) and the new Promat which has superior strength and elasticity. They also sell liquid diluent and liquid sculpey which can be used for molding. You must order by the case.

Powders and Glitters

1. Crescent Bronze Powder Co.
   3400 N. Avondale
   Chicago, IL 60618
   312 539-2441

This company carries 86 different bronze and aluminum powders that can be ordered in bulk or in one ounce amounts. Call to request a sample card.

2. Jean Teten Creations
   5 Broadway Ave.
   Kentfield, CA 94904
   415 453-2989

Jean Tetan carries a huge selection of very fine glitters. He is a wholesaler only and the beginning order is fairly large, but the products are wonderful.

3. Daniel Smith
   4130 First Avenue South
   Seattle, WA 98134-2303
   1-800-426-6740

Daniel Smith carries a selection of interference pigments which are powdered micas, the kind that are used in cosmetics as well as metallic powders, a selection of oil pastels, beautiful papers and other art supplies.

4. Lee S. McDonald, Inc.
   P.O. Box 264
   Charlestown, MA 02129
   617 242-2505
   FAX 617 242-8825

This company is a supplier for papermakers. They carry a wonderful series of pearlescent pigments (mica powders) which are designed to be used with paper pulps but work beautifully as surface powders for polymer clay. They also carry a selection of glitters.

5. United States Bronze Powders, Inc.
   Distributed by:
   Bob Corey Associates
   P.O. Box 73
   1108 Merrick Ave.
   516 485-5544

They distribute 29 different metallic powders. Call to ask for a color card.

6. Gold's Artworks, Inc.
   2100 N.Pine St.
   Lumberton, NC 28358
   800 356-2306

Gold's is a supplier for papermakers. They carry gold and silver leaf among many other items.

7. Golden Artist Colors, Inc.
   Bell Rd.
   New Berlin, NY 13411
   607 847-6154

Golden is a manufacturer of high quality acrylic paints. They make iridescent and interference color acrylics. They also sell acrylic polymer gels which dry clear and make excellent varnishes. It is well worth sending for their color swatches and information on paint safety.

8. New York Central Art Supply
   62 Third Avenue
   New York, NY 10003
   800 950-6111

New York Central is one of the premier art suppliers in the country. They handle products from all over the world. Call for a collection of their catalogs.

Tools and Findings

1. Jerryco Inc.
   601 Linden Place
   Evanston, Ill 60202
   312 475-8440

This is one of my favorite catalogs. Jerryco is a surplus company, but one with a difference! All of the items are written up in great detail and with a lot of humor. If the item is junky, they tell it like it is. I'm listing them because they carry dental picks, pin chucks, sometimes marble rolling pins, and a myriad of other potential "tools" and texturing materials. Their stock of items changes from month to month and year to year but that's part of the fun. Everyone who sees this catalog loves it. A must for all artists!

2. Rio Grande
   6901 Washington, N.E.
   Albuquerque, NM 87109
   800 545-6566

Rio Grande is a jewelers' supplier. They sell an enormous variety of jeweler's tools, findings, metals, and marketing supplies as well as display items, tags and packaging supplies. The definitive catalog for jewelry supply.

3. TSI, Inc.
   101 Nickerson St.
   P.O. Box 9266
   Seattle, WA 98109
   800 426-9984

TSI supplies jewelry making supplies, findings, and beads. They also sell Fimo and many related supplies for working with polymer clays.

4. Thomas Scientific
   99 High Hill Rd.
   I-295 Box 99
   Swedesboro, NJ 08085-0099
   800 345-2100

This company is the only source that I have found for the very fine tissue slicing blades described in the tool chapter. The catalog number is #6727-C20 for a box of 10 blades at $12.45. They also come in a case of 100 for $108.00, catalog #6727-C23.

5. Ornamental Resources
   P.O. Box 3010
   1427 Miner St.
   Idaho Springs, CO 80452
   303 567-4987

Ornamental Resources is a supplier of beads and findings, cording, tassels, sew- on ornaments, rhinestones and much, much more. They are primarily a mail-order business and have an extensive and wonderful catalog which is updated regularly. They are extremely friendly and helpful folks. There is a yearly fee for the catalog and it is well worth it. This catalog is another must if you are making jewelry or are into collage.

6. Tandy Leather Co.
   P.O. Box 791
   Fort Worth, TX 76101

Tandy's is a leather and leather tool supplier. They sell a large selection of leather stamping tools. With over 300 locations nationwide, you may be able to find a store in your region.

7. Woodcraft
   41 Atlantic Ave.
   P.O. Box 4000
   Woburn, MA 01888
   800 225-1153

Woodcraft is a mail order woodworking tool supplier. They carry a wide variety of potentially useful tools for clay working as well as traditional wood tools.

8. Mimi's Books and Supplies for the Serious Dollmaker
   P.O. Box 662
   Point Pleasant, NJ 08742
   201 899-0804

Mimi's carries supplies for dollmaking and related books. Their catalog C 10, Winter 1989/90 has an article by Gloria Winer about working with Polymer Clay which is excellent and well worth requesting.

101. Two whimsical *Mermoo's and a Sea Sow*. Made by Mary Huart Mazer, these figures have shells, chain and jewels as collage elements.

Other Sources Of Inspiration

Periodicals

1. Ornament
   P.O. Box 35029
   Los Angeles, CA 90035-0029
   213 652-9914

Ornament Magazine is a wonderful source of inspiration for artists of all media. They have published numerous articles featuring polymer clay artists and describing related techniques in other media. (see references) I consider this publication a must! Published quarterly for $25.00 per year.

2. American Craft
   American Craft Council
   40 W. 53rd St.
   New York, NY 10019
   212 956-3535

American Craft is a beautiful publication covering contemporary crafts in all media. Membership to the American Crafts Council is $40.00 per year and includes a subscription to the magazine.

3. The Crafts Report
   700 Orange St.
   Wilmington, DE 19801
   302 656-2209

This publication is a must for those of you who are selling your work. The $19.25 per year is well worth it.

4. Rubberstampmadness
   RSM Enterprises
   P.O. Box 6585
   420 Geneva St.
   Ithaca, NY 14851
   607 277-5431

This newspaper format publication is about rubber stamps. There is great information about stamps and stamp suppliers. If you are going to be using stamping with clay, check out this publication. Its great.

5. Dollcrafter
   Scott Publications
   30595 West Eight Mile Rd.
   Livonia, MI 48152
   800 458-8237

This magazine is about dollmaking techniques and has published numerous articles featuring dollmakers working with polymer clays.

6. Threads
   The Taunton Press, Inc.
   63 S. Main St.
   Newtown, CT 06470-5506
   203 426-8171

Threads is a marvelous publication with articles about many different fiber techniques. Though not about polymer clay, there will be information, techniques and possible applications that can be gleaned from this publication. Subscription is $22.00 per year.

7. Fine Woodworking
   The Taunton Press, Inc.
   63 S. Main St.
   Newtown, CT. 06470-5506
   203 426-8171

A great magazine covering many aspects of woodworking. Marquetry, laminating, and carving are just some of the inspirational techniques that may be applied to working with polymer clay. Subscription is $18.00 per year.

9. American Ceramics
   15 West 44 Street
   New York, NY 10036
   212 944-2180

Published quarterly this periodical is the primary resource for ceramicists. Subscription is $28.00 per year.

10. Artspace: A Magazine of Contemporary Art
    P.O. 4547
    Albuquerque, NM 87196
    505 842-1560

A wonderful magazine of art from the west. Subscription rate is $23.00 per year.

11. Fiberarts
    Nine Press
    50 College Street
    Asheville, NC 28801
    704 253-0467

Subscription rates are $24.00 per year. Great publication for what is happening in the fiber world.

12. New Work: Glass
    New York Experimental Glass Workshop
    142 Mulberry Street
    New York, NY 10013

A publication featuring contemporary glass artists. Subscription is $15.00 per year.

Organizations

1. The Polymer Clay Guild
   c/o Lindly Miller & Pat Berlin
   928 Mackall Ave.
   McLean, VA 22101

Dues are $20.00 per year. A newsletter is published 5 times a year and all are invited to join, submit articles, information and announcements. The Guild's mission is to gather and disseminate information on polymer clays and to promote the media through exhibits. A slide bank is in preparation for rental by groups.

2. The Bead Society of Greater Washington
   P.O. Box 70036
   Chevy Chase, MD 20088-0036
   301 656-9255

At current writing, there are 15 bead societies nationwide. Many of them are listed in Ornament Magazine. While the organization focuses on beads primarily, jewelry and ornamentation of all kinds are studied and discussed.

3. National Institute of American Doll Artists (NIADA)
   Susanna Oroyan
   1880 Parliament St.
   Eugene, OR 97405

The touchstone organization for doll artists nationally.

4. Penland School of Crafts
   Penland, NC 28765
   704 765-2359

One of the oldest as most respected craft schools in the country. Ceramics, metals and glassworking are just a few of the disciplines taught. A wonderful place!

5. Touchstone Center for Crafts
   P.O. Box 2141
   Uniontown, PA 15401
   1 800 753-2733

A relatively new (7 years old), summer arts colony.

Footnotes

1. For more information, see **The History of Beads** by Lois Sherr Dubin. Abrams, 1987

2. See the references by John Coyne and Ban Kajitani on page131.

3. See R. K. Liu, *The Bead Journal*, 1(4):24-41, 1975. "Faience: Technical Aspects and Beads of Simple Form."

4. From **The Elements of Color**, Johannes Itten, page 52. Van Nostrand Reinhold, 1970

5. From **The Seminole Patchwork Book** by Cheryl Bradkin.

6. From **Jewelry Concepts & Technology** by Oppi Untracht.

7. All cylinders are "canes", patterned or not, though plain canes are often called "rods" by glassworkers.

8. "Cray-pas" & "Nupastels" are trade names for oil based pigments in stick form used to draw on canvas or paper.

9. See the references by Burgess, R. H. and Sarvetnick, H.